TAYOZAAN

THE PHYSICAL WORLDS AND ZERO WORLDS

For Ben, Galina and
Beatrice
Love to your lives!
Noor and Olive August 1999

TAYOZAAN
THE PHYSICAL WORLDS AND ZERO WORLDS

Published by Noor Hasan 1998

ISBN: 0 9516012 1 0

TAYOZAAN
THE PHYSICAL WORLDS AND ZERO WORLDS
is a revised and fully amplified version of
"TAYOZAAN – THE FOURTH BEGINNING"
(the first commitment to writing of the
Philosophy of TAYOZAAN) published in
England, U.K. by Noor Hasan in 1990.

Printed in England, U.K.
by O'Reilly Clark of Enfield, Middlesex

INDEX

FROM THE AUTHOR

TAYOZAAN is a Philosophy for Life; a philosophy which has progressively come to be what it is as at this point in time as a result of a succession of personal experiences.

The actual practical Systems of TAYOZAAN began to be formulated in London, England, in the early Summer of 1976, since when the whole philosophy has continued to evolve – within the stresses and imperfections of a very ordinary existence – with extraordinary speed and dynamism. It has therefore taken twenty-two years of development to enable this book to be written. The first thirteen of those years took place in midst of my working life. And it took those thirteen years for the very name of TAYOZAAN to come to be.

There is no joy in keeping knowledge for oneself alone. The beauty of my life lies in the fulfilment of the many. I therefore dedicate this book to all humanity.

I also wish to record my gratitude to Great Britain, the land in which the Philosophy of TAYOZAAN has found its destined expression.

NOOR HASAN
DECEMBER 1998

The author Noor Hasan with his wife and co-author Olive Hasan

In the most difficult of conquests the first act is the thought ***"I will!"***

PRELIMINARY
TO THE
BOOK OF TAYOZAAN

MYTHOLOGICAL TALES

The Story of the God Kikalva

The spirit Kikalva cast his eyes around the Earth until his attention fastened on a remote island in the tropical seas on which lived two youths: a young male named Zedan and a young female named Laleya. They were the island's sole human inhabitants. They lived on nuts and fruits garnered from the lush fertile vegetation of their sun-washed land – and they were happy together, carefree and innocent. They shared the exotic beauties and warmth of their island with the animals and birds.

Having viewed this situation, the spirit Kikalva saw it was ideal for his purpose and during the night he entered into the dreams of Zedan. Kikalva appeared to him in beauteous form in an aura of delicate colours and dazzling light. He spoke to Zedan in a voice of crystal clarity and charm – the sweetest voice Zedan had ever heard; a voice of persuasive quality. He said: "I am thy God Kikalva. I created you and your wife Laleya and your island which I have called the Island of Dream. In the beginning I caused this land to rise from the depths of the wide ocean and I fashioned it, forming its majestic mountains and its verdant valleys. I caused crystal waters to cascade from rocky precipice to deep blue lagoons beneath. I shaped the lakes and rivers and made its many kinds of trees, shrubs and flowers. It is I who created the exotic vegetation which flourishes and bears the multitude of fruits, berries and sweet smelling flowers you now enjoy. I was greatly pleased with my work and brought my Goddess Kalvee to see what I had created, but she said 'Something is lacking. Nothing *moves* except the waters and the trees and grasses which sway in the breeze. There must be more *life*'. So I further thought and in the Autumn of that year I gathered many different shapes of leaves which I placed in valleys beside the lakes and rivers and on the rising of the sun I waved my hands to and fro causing the wind of life to blow with swirling force, sending the leaves up into the sky. As they floated down through the shafts of sunlight, the many kinds of leaf became creatures of the air and waters. So there came to be the many kinds of bird and fowl which have their home amongst the trees and which enjoy the Island's lakes and rivers. And so, likewise, came to be formed the many kinds of fish and other water creatures which inhabit the lakes, rivers and surrounding ocean. And I waved my hands again and they all became fertile with urge to mate and reproduce their kind".

"I was greatly pleased with my work. I called my Goddess Kalvee to admire the wonderful variety of feathered creatures of many hues whose flight and song now filled the Island of Dream and for her to see that the waters also were now teaming with colourful life. She came and beheld and agreed that it was indeed all very admirable, but she said: 'But nothing moves on the *Earth*'. So I thought again, and in the summer of the next year I returned and gathered fallen branches and twigs of wood from a variety of trees which I placed in a sheltered Valley. Again I waited until sunrise. I then began to walk on the pieces of wood, the branches and twigs which I had gathered together, massaging them with my feet. The warmth and sweat of my feet blended into the different kinds of wood of various thicknesses and size and I moulded them into the great variety of animals which now inhabit the Island of Dream. And as the sun rose higher in the sky and the heat from the sun's rays increased, the animals matured into adult beasts ready to reproduce their kind in a loving, caring way, befitting me their Creator who is a loving, caring God".

"I saw that the Island of Dream was now excitingly alive and I was overjoyed at my creation. I immediately summoned my Goddess again to view my works and she too showed her pleasure. But again she was not totally satisfied and said: 'I see that some of the animals are more intelligent than others but cannot you make an animal with much more intelligence, with whom we can speak?' So, after long further thought I decided on a way to make a special creature whom I determined should be called "man"; and in the middle of the next summer I returned again to the Island of Dream with the sole intention of creating this animal of higher intelligence to finalise my work. I prepared a special place on the mountainside from which there was a glorious vista over the whole terrain of the Island and amongst the flowers in a protected cleft I placed two special pieces of stick, side by side. One was knobbly and long. The other was smooth and short. And on the evening of the rise of the full moon I took hold of the short smooth piece of wood and began to stroke and massage it with my hands. The warmth and sweat of my hands softened and moulded the stick to form the shape of a beautiful young woman. This, Zedan, was your wife Laleya, whom I created. I caused her to go into a deep sleep to await your coming. The following day at break of dawn I took hold of the longer, knobbly stick and with stronger strokes massaged it with my hands until my warmth and sweat made it pliable; and I formed it into the shape of a young man – into you, Zedan, whom I also caused to go into deep sleep. And while you slept I imbued you both with intelligence and with the knowledge of communication between yourselves. I also gave you the ability to commune with the animals. I then went away and awoke you both from afar. I took away from you any memory of myself."

Having spoken thus, the spirit Kikalva said: "I leave you now, Zedan, but you now know that I am your God, your Creator. And I will return again to your dreams ..."

That morning when Zedan awoke, the memory of his dreams came flooding back to him and he was filled with joy and exhilaration. Never before had he had vision of such a Being nor been told such a wonderful story; and he hastened to tell Laleya of his dream. She too was full of wonder and they were radiantly happy to know they had a loving God who had now made himself known to them and was coming into their lives. To be joined by a Being of greater intelligence than the animals who until then had been their only company was a thrilling event and as this Being was, moreover, their very Creator, their trusting hearts felt a wonderful sense of security. To make their happiness even greater, Laleya told Zedan she was with child. She and Zedan ran to share their joy with the Island. They frolicked in the spray of the waterfall and swam, diving deep into the clear blue waters to tell the fish of their joy. They then ran through woods and valleys carpeted with wild flowers, drying themselves under the hot sun, singing aloud, irradiating their happiness to the birds and their other animal friends.

Amongst the closest of Zedan and Laleya's animal friends were the dog, the horse and the cow. The cow was the wisest of the animals on the Island and their best friend.

The months went by and in the Spring, shortly before Laleya was due to give birth, Kikalva returned to Zedan's dreams. He said: "A son will be born to you whose name shall be 'Afdan'. This further joy I bestow on you. My Goddess Kalvee and I have observed your happiness. We have watched your enjoyment of all the bounty of this

Island which I made for you. And now, to show your gratitude, at time of every full moon I want you and Laleya to make a burnt offering of thanks and praise to me. Go to the forest at the east of the Island where you will find a tree standing alone whose bark is scented. Take the bark of this tree, go to the special place on the mountainside where I created you and on a table which you must make as altar for me you must burn the perfumed bark in my honour... for my enjoyment... for the smell is pleasing to me. You must also at regular intervals burn some of this bark in your home out of respect for me. The smoke and the perfume will be token of your esteem. Also each morning at first light you must dedicate your lives to me - and to me alone, for I am a jealous God – and go to the base of the mountain where two rocks stand, one taller than the other. You, Zedan, must stand upon the taller rock and Laleya must stand upon the shorter rock. You shall each of you make obeisance to me and sing my praises. Acknowledge me to be your Creator, God above all Gods. Tell me I am beauteous and all powerful and that you fear me – and I will continue to look favourably upon you both and your yet unborn son. Do not question my commands. In fact I command that neither you nor Laleya ever question WHY?"

On awakening Zedan told Laleya of this further dream. They were delighted to know she would bear a son and they duly did as Kikalva required by making him burnt offerings of sweet-smelling bark on the mountainside and in their home. They also performed the daily ritual of adoration and submission required by Kikalva, as he had commanded. And in due course Laleya gave birth to a male child whom they called "Afdan" as they had been bidden.

Afdan grew into a beautiful child. He was strong, sensitive and intelligent. Afdan spent much time with the Island's animals whom he loved. The bees gave him their honey and their especial friend, the wise cow, gave freely of her milk for his succour. Zedan and Laleya greatly loved their son.

One day when Afdan was some two years old, Zedan returned from his travels to the east coast to obtain scented bark and from making the ritual burnt offering upon the mountainside, and he was silent, in deep thought. Laleya asked him if he were troubled. "I do not understand" said Zedan "why the God Kikalva should need us to keep destroying his beautiful trees with the sweet smelling bark, for I have had to find many such trees now to fulfil his command and without their bark they die. It makes me so sad to injure the trees and see them die. How can he, who has made everything, need me to do this and find it pleasing? And why does he need to be told how wonderful and all powerful he is and that we respect him? Surely he must know, as he made us, what is in our hearts and that we honour and love him without having to carry out this ritual?" Laleya was disturbed by Zedan's words and said "Zedan, be careful. Is not this questioning Why? which God Kikalva told us we must never do? Let us go and talk with the wise cow and see what she advises". But night was descending and they decided to visit their friend the wise cow the next morning.

That night Kikalva appeared in Laleya's dreams. He was in rage. His eyes were frightening and she shivered with an icy coldness. Kikalva told her that Zedan had broken his command by questioning it and that by way of atonement and penance they must kill their friend, the wise cow who was close to their hearts, and offer its body as burnt sacrifice at the special place on the mountainside. "The smell of burnt flesh is especially pleasing to me and will placate my wrath" he said. "Do this if you honour me". As Kikalva removed himself from her dreams his final fading words were: "If you disobey my command and do not make this sacrifice to me before time of the next full moon, you son will die".

Laleya awoke with a scream, her heart rent, her mind full of fear. When she told Zedan, with tears raining down her face, her experience of the night, he at first did not wish to believe her. He wished to think it was only a bad dream, a nightmare caused by her anxieties over his own disquieting thoughts; but Laleya convinced him it was not merely a dream but a visitation from Kikalva within her dreams. This Zedan recognised from his own experience ... and so he and Laleya straightaway and in anxious haste went to see the wise cow. They told her the whole story from the time of the first visitation of Kikalva into Zedan's dreams.

The wise cow listened quietly and then said: "Kikalva is not your God. He has not created you. He has lied to you Zedan and your son will not die if you do not serve him – but the more you bow down to the spirit Kikalva the more power he will have over you and the greater will be your bondage. But he cannot have power over you and make you do what is offensive to your heart if you do not agree to his commands and if you have faith in your own deep conscience and love. If you kill me and make sacrifice of me you may placate his anger now, but it will not stop there. He will want you to build a great temple in his honour. He will want you to make more and more blood sacrifices. He will not be satisfied until you submit your Will entirely to him. But should you allow that, Zedan, he will possess you. He wants your soul. The precious Light of your Life will be more and more obscured until it shrivels and becomes paralysed. Like a fly in the spider's web you will feel unable to free yourself. Under Kikalva's domination you will become the mere plaything of the forces of darkness; and even after death his power over you will not diminish". The wise cow sighed and said: "Kikalva hates wisdom. It is a threat to him. It is a threat to his domination ... And so he hates me and wishes to destroy me".

Having heard these words Zedan was greatly moved. He said: "My dear friend, you have opened my eyes. How could I possibly agree to commit such a crime against you? I will *not* carry out Kikalva's command. But I fear for my son. It is known that you can see into the future. Tell me, what will happen to Afdan?" The wise cow replied: "Be at peace. Have no fear for your son. I see him maturing into a fine young man – strong, capable and kind – and in his manhood he will find a way to leave this Island. He will come to meet his destined mate in another land and you will have two grandchildren."

Thus reassured, Zedan arose and set out for the mountains. He climbed to the special place where the altar had been made and called upon Kikalva who immediately appeared before him – for with the cunning awareness of his spirit Kikalva already knew he had been recognised and that he was being opposed by Zedan – and he was there ere his name had left Zedan's lips. He appeared on a clap of thunder, with frightening countenance, swelled to gigantic girth. A mass of black cloud obscured the sunlight, a wind arose which whined and shrieked in violent gusts like some demented creature, whipping eddies of dank mist about the darkened rocks; and a chill of more than mere coldness gripped Zedan. His small frame was dwarfed by the bleak mountainous crags. A powerful evil atmosphere pervaded his nervous system. Kikalva was penetrating his mind and heart with a great fear to subjugate him into obeisance. "You cannot resist my power, Zedan" cried Kilalva. "Accept me as your Master. You need me. You have no choice".

Zedan had never before felt such darkness of soul. Never before had he known the grip of such fear. He was transfixed. He was sorely tempted to succumb in weakness. His knees buckled beneath him and he slumped to the ground. He felt vulnerable and lost; but as he desperately searched within himself for some initiative to take him out of his self-doubting turmoil, he realised that a part of him remained as silent witness to his own drama, like an immovable light – a part within the depth of his being which was beyond harm. At the same time Zedan recalled the words of his friend the wise cow: *"He cannot have power over you ... if you do not agree to his commands and if you have faith in your own deep conscience and love"*.

So, with all his night, like a man drowning at sea who grasps at a saving oar, Zedan gathered his forces to that inviolable place of witness within himself; and as he did so he felt Kikalva's power over him diminish. The more strongly he held on to his own inner sense of Being the more rapidly did the fear which had overwhelmed him recede.

Zedan raised himself from his knees until he stood erect. He voiced his realisation aloud: "You cannot have power over me, Kikalva. I do not agree with your commands. My faith is in the Light of my Life"... And as Zedan was filled with yet greater confidence of faith in himself, he shouted: "Kikalva. I am my own Master and I will not succumb to you. I will be Master over your dark force!"

Kikalva roared and smote Zedan with his power again and again but Zedan stood firm, continuing to challenge him with increasing strength, fending Kikalva's force with his own like a magical shield; and Zedan realised that as his unswerving determination strengthened, not only could he parry the blows but he could strike back with his own force. So Zedan mustered all the power of his Being and fought the darkness. As he did so he saw that Kikalva was rapidly losing his power and the fiercesome gigantic form he had projected was reducing in size.

"Kikalva" exulted Zedan "I see you now for what you are. You are not our Creator. You are false. No longer will I be deceived. But through you I have come to know where lies my real strength; I have seen the value of my true Self. I now know the way I must go. I will tell my son so that he and his children will have this truth I have now seen".

Upon hearing this, with a coarse final cry Kikalva's diminishing spirit evaporated into extinction, his energies reabsorbed into the elements; and as Zedan's power triumphed, a blue triangular shaft of Light – a light not as of this world – beamed from Zedan's brow, blessing the whole area whereon he stood.

Zedan stood for a time in the quiet appreciation of his own uplifted state. He knew his efforts had earned him a higher substance of Being. The winds which had accompanied Kikalva's presence rapidly eased to a gentle breath, the dark clouds lifted, the air was once again full of birdsong and the flowers irradiated their beauty once more. The mountains were restored to a sublime tranquillity, reflecting Zedan's own newfound exalted state; and the sun shimmered in acknowledgment of his victory.

Zedan left the mountains, hastening back to his loved ones. He was strong with courage; his Being filled with a wonderful sense of love – and gratitude. He knew that his soul had matured. He knew that he must share his new dawning with Laleya and Afdan; and he knew that from thenceforth their lives would be lived in the light of a new understanding, with a new sense of purpose in a new kind of freedom. He would question "**Why**?" and become wise.

THE MYTH OF OMEYA

The land of Omeya was beautiful in terrain and fertile but its people were dejected in spirit for they were ruled by the tyrannical and treacherous King Dassa. The injustices of his rule brought great hardship on the people, especially to the peasant farmers whose labours were exploited. The heavy taxes which King Dassa imposed kept them impoverished, and they could see no escape, no hope of change whilst they remained under his oppressive rule.

Then one day a man named Vantona was reported to be going through the streets of Omeya proclaiming: "A Saviour is coming! A Saviour is coming!" The people were eager to hear more, Their hopes were raised but they wanted to know how Vantona – who was just an ordinary peasant like themselves – could possibly know that the so long awaited Saviour was actually coming at last to the land of Omeya. Vantona enjoyed finding himself the centre of attention. He explained that whilst he was herding his cattle in the remote pastureland, he heard a Voice which told him he must go to the people of Omeya and tell them "A Saviour is coming". He said that at first he doubted his own senses and thought it was but the sound of the wind, but that he heard the Voice again several times and eventually he put aside his further fears that he might be being misled by an evil Spirit and he decided to do as he was bidden – in the hopes that the Voice spoke the truth.

The people of Omeya believed Vantona to be honest and they very much wanted to believe the message of the Voice. They had faith that God was at last about to extend his hand to end their suffering, and they were overjoyed.

New hope blossomed in the hearts of the people of Omeya – but sadly, season after season went by. Year after year went by. Vantona had grown old. And still the Saviour had not come. Hardship and gloom overcame the peasants as they found themselves coming yet further under the domination of the uncaring King Dassa, and the people eventually lost belief in Vantona and the message of the Voice.

Then one very fine day, a peasant rode in on a galloping horse crying: "The Saviour has come! The Saviour has come! He is in the City". Great excitement swept through the villages and a group of Elders went straight away to give the news to the disconsolate Vantona who lived alone and was now very old. The Elders told Vantona of the people's remorse and shame at having disbelieved him and having eventually treated him badly because the Saviour had taken so long to come; but that they now honoured Vantona for he had in fact spoken the truth.

News of the coming of the Saviour had reached the ears of the wicked King Dassa whose only concern was to retain power over the people. He had no respect for the Saviour, nor did he believe the Saviour could do anything to free the peasants from his domination – but he hurriedly ordered his Army to humiliate and arrest the Saviour since he would be easy to locate in the City.

However, days passed with no word from his Generals. All King Dassa could see were signs of jubilation in the streets surrounding his Palace. So he sent his Emissaries to report to him what was happening. He awaited their news in a state of great agitation and demanded they be brought before him without ceremony immediately they returned.

On their return the Emissaries somewhat fearfully presented themselves before the King. Wide of eye they haltingly told him that when the soldiers were about to arrest the Saviour he jumped into the mighty River Gandana. And began to push at the river bank, whereupon half of the City had parted from the mainland causing the course of the river to divide and surround that part of the City on which were arrayed the soldiers of King Dassa's Army. Half of the City had therefore become an island surrounded by the deep waters of the mighty River Gandana, and without vessels to aid them the soldiers were marooned. Moreover, beholding such miraculous powers, the soldiers were now afraid of the Saviour, who remained on the mainland unharmed.

King Dassa was most disquieted and angered at the failure of his Generals, but being a cunning man, he composed himself and with the help of his closest advisers, his soothsayers and astrologers, he thought up a plan to ensnare the Saviour and secure his death.

Word that King Dassa had a secret plan to slay the Saviour reached the ears of the aging peasant Vantona. So great was his concern at this news that he set off immediately in his bullock cart to the plain where he had first heard the Voice which told him of the Saviour's coming. Vantona fell to his knees on the windswept grasslands where his cattle had grazed on that memorable day so many years before, and raising his eyes to the skies he besought help from the Voice to tell him what needed to be done to help the Saviour; but there was no reply. With sad heart the old man begged the Voice to save the Saviour from any harm. He pleaded that the Saviour might live to free the people of Omeya from their bondage. But still there was only silence. As time of sunset neared, a group of women passed by. Seeing the old man on his knees and hearing his pleas they told Vantona that it was too late, that the Saviour had already met his death; that he had been killed on the command of King Dassa.

Vantona was overwhelmed by grief and disappointment. Tremulously he cried out for the Voice to speak. He beat his breast and cried to the sky again and again; and at last, in the late evening, the Voice answered. It said "Do not despair. The Saviour's spirit is still alive. Only his body is dead". The Voice continued: "Tell your people to drive a square silver bar, six feet in length, into the ground. Each morning, before sunrise, they must strike the silver bar six times and make a square sign on their chests. The sound will awaken the Saviour whose spirit is alive in the earth and the people can ask him for help. Know that he is your Saviour who will always be alive under your feet and when you make the square sign on your chest he will protect you in this World".

Vantona asked in amazement "Why should the people need to do such a strange thing?" The Voice replied: "King Dassa so feared the Saviour – so feared that he would come to usurp his own authority – that he sought a way to destroy him. As well as deliberating with his astrologers and Shamans, he consulted his Oracle. The Oracle looked into the future and saw that the Saviour would need to be slain in a special way if his miraculous powers were to be overcome. And so plans were laid to overcome the Saviour. Under the darkness of night at a time when the clouds were so dense that they obscured not only the full moon but even the light of the stars, King Dassa's henchmen, in the guise of holy seekers, moved stealthily and silently to where the Saviour lay sleeping and slew him. He was killed by six blows. A square silver bar was then driven through his chest. That is the special way in which the Saviour died. And that is why in future the people of Omeya must make contact with his spirit in the way I have commanded".

The Voice spoke no more. Darkness descended and all was silent.

With great heaviness of heart Vantona passed the message of the Voice to the people of Omeya and strange though it may seem, their hearts and minds were satisfied. And although all the many and diverse sufferings of their lives continued just as before, the Omeyan Priests and the people: the old, the young, the bereaved, the sick... those in need of solace or protection and those who sought special favours from the Saviour...believed – and believe to this day – that in all places and at all times throughout their lives, if they make the sign of the square on their chests they are connected with the Saviour; for the Voice told them that the spirit of the Saviour still lives.

THE
BOOK OF TAYOZAAN

PART ONE

FACE TO FACE WTH THE UNUTTERABLE/BRAHMAN

My memories, from early childhood onwards, are richly laden with experiences of other-worldly nature.

This **Physical World** which we inhabit is but one layer of a multi-dimensional Reality. No doubt most of us will readily agree that beyond the physical body our real sense of Selfhood lies within us, in the internal realm of our mind and feelings. This internal realm belongs to a different dimensional reality from that of the physical. In the language of the philosophy of TAYOZAAN, it belongs to the reality of the **Zero Worlds**: that whole multi-depthed dimensional zone which is connected to, is within, but yet is also beyond the Physical Worlds of Existence.

The "Zeroness" of the Zero Worlds is a *Nothingness* but it is only a "Nothingness" in terms of comparison with this gross world of physical matter.

Within the physical body is its spirit natured counterpart: that which is as it were the inner blueprint of the physical form. It is of the more subtle internal level which TAYOZAAN has named the **Stabilising Dimension**. This inner level of our Being is therefore also referred to as our *Stabilising* ***Self***. Our mind and the emotions it generates are also of that Stabilising dimensional nature.

However, as the reader will also no doubt recognise to be true, our most intense sense of Selfhood lies within the very depth of our mind and heart, beyond the more or less superficial functioning of our brain and emotions. And indeed this is so, as yet deeper within us is the Light of ***Life*** itself: our creative force, of indestructible nature; that which belongs to the dimension named by TAYOZAAN the **Unutterable Dimension**. That *Life* which we are is therefore also referred to as our *Unutterable* ***Self***.

The Unutterable Dimension is the **Brahman** level of Aryan Hinduism, the dimension of creativity from which **Existence**, the material Worlds of matter, came to Be.

The "Unutterable" Dimension is so named as when first experienced I could not speak of it at all. The experience itself was so extraordinary, so overwhelming in its impact, that it left me temporarily speechless. I was literally unable to utter a word. Actually there is no language in our human vocabulary to adequately describe what it is for there is nothing within manifest Existence with which the Unutterable dimensional reality can be compared. That internal dimension is supra physical. It is of a totally different nature to that of the Physical Worlds.

When but a little boy, my days were many times peopled by spirits from the Stabilising Dimension. Being so young I had no idea then that this was in any way unusual.

These spirits were sometimes in the form of children; some were fully gown. Some had beautiful bodies but showed no heads. These Stabilising forms would often project themselves into my awareness as I played alone. I was pleased to have their company, especially at times when I was particularly sad, hurt and lonely – for as a child I was many times subjected to physical violence as well as intense mental and emotional abuse. My father terrorised me – as he did my mother and other members of our famiiy – but his wrath was mainly directed towards me. Small as I was, I tried to protect my Mother – which did not help my own situation. In fact I was beaten so badly that my hearing was damaged. Although by nature a happy child, full of energy and quick to laughter, many times the violence left me traumatised – by pain and stark fear – and deeply unhappy.

During those years these Beings of the Stabilising Dimension would join me in my solitude or in my play. They would come and go, departing just as unexpectedly and swiftly as they had arrived; always leaving me with a sense of happiness and comfort. I was not, therefore, at all frightened by them but found solace from their presence even into my later years – until I learned, and in time more clearly understood, the dangers inherent in allowing close connection with the spirit world. In fact I paid dearly in later years for permitting the closeness of one such beautiful "spirit" who befriended me and on whose solace I came to depend.

I now know that there are millions of "shades" or selves of the Stabilising Dimension which exist for a time after death of the physical body; the physical body's death being when it is no longer animated by its Stabilising and Unutterable content.

I also now know that the Unutterable Light, the real *Life* of the individual, can be reborn into a new body even while its former Stabilising Self or "personality" exists on for a time in the Stabilising Dimension. Therefore even though a familiar form of a deceased loved one is seen after death, one is not necessarily in contact with the true Self of Unutterable Light of that person. What one sees may well only be that energised psyche, that blueprint of the physical body – the Stabilising Self –

which is able to continue for a while after leaving its physical body.

However, as these forms can also be produced – "manufactured" – by the dark, opposing Anti Life Forces to deceive us, it is wise not to invite connection with the spirit world at all. Above all, never open yourselves to allow them to enter or possess you.

As it is such a potentially dangerous area, it is in fact best to leave the Stabilising field strictly alone, in the understanding that whilst we are indeed of and connected with all Life's dimensions, the task of each of us is to direct our interest and energies towards maturing the Unutterable Light of Life within our own Being. Our protection lies in that which is our true Self coming to assume full possession and control of itself.

* * * *

Over the years there have been further experiences of other-worldly nature which are indelibly imprinted on my memory for the effect of those further experiences has been truly transforming.

There have been occasions when the depth of my Being, that is my own Unutterable Light, has connected acutely with the Unutterable nature of the world. I have "seen", "felt", its unique internal dimensional *atmosphere*, been imbued with its Unutterable quality of Love: such an intensity of Love... a Love which both emanated from and irradiated the whole area where I happened to be at the time. Trees, shrubs, flowers; the buildings, street lamps... even old tin cans and rubbish... were full of it. The soil, the dirt underfoot were alive with its indescribably glorious vibration which remained within my Being for some time after the happening came to an end.

However, although an incredibly wonderful experience, such quality and intensity of Love I found too strong, too much for my nervous system to bear for more than a short while. I could not concentrate, nor therefore could I give full attention to my work whilst it remained with me – and I just had to get on with my life – so that when the intense vibration faded from my being by degrees over the next few days, I was relieved. I felt more at peace; glad to have returned to my former state of "normality".

From time to time there have also been visitations from Zero Beings of deeper dimensional nature. An Unutterable Being is seen whether the eyes be open or closed. The "seeing" is with internal vision. The "eye" which is capable of beholding must be of similar Zero nature within the viewer to that which is beholden. When such viewing – of and from the Zero dimensions – takes place, although that which is seen is external to oneself when the physical eyes are open, it is still seen by one's internal vision even when the physical eyes are closed.

As has been explained, the "Unutterable" level has been so called because it cannot really be described. And for some time I could not even attempt to speak of it. As a child, when I experienced the Beings or state of the Unutterable Dimension, it was so extraordinary, so strangely different from my encounters with the spirits and state of the Stabilising Dimension that, despite the brutish ignorance of his nature, I would run to find my father, wanting so much to tell him what had happened and seek his explanation; for my father was a Muslim and I felt sure he would understand what it was. However, although I rushed with breathless excitement to find my father, before I could reach him the whole experience would suddenly leave me and I would find myself bereft of speech; quite unable to say anything about it.

Although too young on those occasions to understand much at all, I knew I was experiencing something quite exceptional.

Despite its quality of "Nothingness" – a state devoid of anything our ordinary human experience can relate to – that Zero quality is a vital, *living* and *qualitied* emptiness. That other-worldly atmosphere of the Unutterable, that qualitied emptiness, is also a living *Silence*; a Silence of such penetrating intensity, one is "deafened" by it. One's ordinary state of being is both permeated and suffused by it.

On occasions an Unutterable Being and/or the atmosphere or nature of the Unutterable Dimension has been experienced as a Light of cloudy whiteness but which yet at the same time is transparent. Although it is a Nothingness, at the same time it conveys a certain "solidity" for it has substance of its own dimensional quality. It is outside and yet inside of one at the same time, it being both seen and felt. One is as it were locked within a globule of experience of its other worldly quality.

The Unutterable Being whose Light of this quality had come to me when I was a child appeared then to be both observing and knowing me. And I knew that the Unutterable Light who visited me from time to time during the subsequent period of my boyhood was the same Being who had made Himself known to me when I was younger.

As I grew into teenage, amongst those whom I viewed as friends were several men and women (much older than myself) who were longtime spiritualists. I therefore ventured to relate my experience of this Unutterable Being to one such friend – whose name was Emanuel, although he was known to us all as "Manny". I reasoned that as a spiritualist he would no doubt be able to recognise such description as I was able to give.

At that time I referred to the Unutterable Being as "Mr Nothing" or "Mr Empty Nothing". However the more I tried to describe to Manny the quality of this Being and its dimensional nature, the less was he able to understand. My experience did not relate to anything he had known. He said he was only aware of apparitions or spirits having form, a recognisable shape. His experiences could always be spoken of, could always be fairly well described. But he could not recognise, nor even conceptualise, what it was I was speaking of.

This came as a shock. It was a great surprise and even greater disappointment to me as I had thought my very good friend Manny to be perhaps the only person with whom I could share such precious personal experience. In fact I had felt quite confident that he, above all people whom I then knew, would understand. He was himself saddened. He wholly believed me but was just unable to recognise such description as I was able to give.

I was therefore alone with my experiences; and thereafter I did make enquiry of anyone else. In fact I spoke to no-one else about them for many years.

* * * *

On an occasion when I was in my early twenties, a Being from the Zero dimensions took human shape before me. At the time I was working at a forest camp in South America, in the then Colony of British Guyana where I was born.

This Being was in male form. He appeared to me whilst I was resting on the river bank. He was white of skin, his attire being I would say of Middle Eastern style. He projected a warm, kindly face; a face full of compassion. His movements as he walked towards me were soft and gentle. I did not see his feet. They were covered by the long grey loose fitting garment which he wore. His headgear was white. He had no beard or moustache. He had hazel coloured eyes.

He "spoke" to me, not in words but through the eyes. It was a direct communication to me with his eyes through my eyes. I could only connect with him by making eye contact, that is through my physical vision, yet it was apparent that our connection was via the internal Stabilising Dimension which enabled us to make direct communication with each other. Thought and feeling could be perfectly and completely conveyed, one to the other, through our eyes.

In this kind of direct connection the *wholeness of* ***meaning*** is immediately conveyed in a way which is quite impossible to effect when communication one to another has to take place through the cumbersome machinery of ordinary language.

I found that the exchange of communication between us stopped if one or other of us looked away or if one of us chose to stop the transmission. The mind could stop communicating through the eyes in just the same way as the mouth can stop talking in ordinary speech communication if one wills it so.

My life had always been difficult but it was particularly so at the time of this visitation. It was apparent that this Being was well aware of my content, of what was in my heart and mind. It was clear that in fact he knew me well.

His eyes were the first to speak. His message to me was one of loving goodwill. It was a message of encouragement for me to go forward, to proceed with my life. I was given assurance that I had his full support for what I had to do.

I did not fully understand at the time that his message of loving support and encouragement was not limited to that particular period of my life but was meant to convey long-term support into the years ahead.

I was tremendously grateful for this Being's visit. It was as though I had been given actual sustenance and balm. The wonderful feeling which accompanied His presence and the vibration of deep Love which He left within me in that forest, lasted a full week.

* * * *

I was in a joyful, loving state following that encounter but I knew then, and have understood many times since, that we must not expect help in the way of intervention from these Beings even at times of deepest need – for once they start to help, the human mind will come to rely on them.

That we do receive support and encouragement from the internal spheres I have no doubt. There has been ample evidence of this at other times of greatest need over the years – for which I have been immensely grateful. But I know that any other kind of direct intervention in the process of our lives would be wrong.

In fact, as we witness, we are not normally helped. Judged from viewpoint of their heirarchical positions in the cosmos, for the Zero Beings to intervene in our lives would be an abnegation of their responsibility towards us for it would undermine human progress. Dependancy upon receiving help produces a vegetative state of mind. Not only would our intelligence and forwarding drive not grow, it would fast decline.

As with reliance upon prayer – which saps and weakens the creative power of our Light – if prayer was answered and everything we sought was granted, our growth on the internal path would be completely stifled. The full potential of our human destiny would be lost to us.

* * * *

I have observed (with vision of Stabilising Dimensional nature) that the Universe which we at present inhabit has its own Ruler.

This Being projected to me the form it had during its last human incarnation. It appeared in female form. She was white of skin and was dressed in a full lengthed, loose fitting dress similar to that of a sari.

This Ruler of our Universe, this "Queen", came with an atmosphere of the East. Her demeanour was one of authority, great dignity and efficiency. She was accompanied by another female who was brown skinned. This other female, who appeared to be the Ruler's companion, began to dance before me with undulating movements. It was a form of dance which also evoked an atmosphere of the East.

This experience was not something that was expected, requested or desired by me but this is what occurred. The happening lasted only a short while in physical time but it was imbued by the uniquely Zero, silent quality of timelessness.

Within the seeing was also a knowing. The white skinned female did not tell me that she is the Ruler of this our own Universe – there being billions of other Universes within the vast Body of Existence, each no doubt with its own internal dimensional Rulers – but in the seeing of her was the knowledge that this is so. I also understood that her abode is in the most brilliant star studded head of the vast fishlike creature or form which I have seen to be the shape of our Universe (referred to in The Cosmology of TAYOZAAN hereafter); that star studded "head" from which she rules being some hundred times brighter than the Universe's centre, the centre in turn being a great deal brighter than the section on one of the fins of this cosmic creature where our own galaxy is positioned.

This experience occurred during a time when I was practising one of the practical Systems of the philosophy of TAYOZAAN which involves the internal acceptance to oneself of this our own Universe in attitude of love and intense gratitude, thus producing a Oneness of Stabilising dimensional nature between oneself and the Being of that whole cosmic creature, a vastly contrary attitude, action – and result – to that of treating this manifest world as illusory or seeking to abandon it – as is the teaching of some philosophical disciplines.

* * * *

I have also seen (this time with internal vision of Unutterable dimensional nature) that our Galaxy within this our own particular Universe is in turn ruled by three Unutterable Beings.

I do not know what these three Unnutterable Beings were in their last incarnations in human form...whether they had been male or female. This was not projected to me but they presented themselves to me during one night as three Unutterable Lights. They were very similar but yet each was quite distinctive one from the other. Their Lights were of the glowing cloudy yet transparent whiteness which I had come to recognise as belonging to Beings of the Unutterable Dimension.

These Beings gave an impression of responsibility and of their high efficiency. I understood that they wished me to know of their position in the Cosmos. This confirmed to me that there is work to be done (albeit of a much different nature) when Beings mature into the eternal Zero dimensions, and that they work within material existence. But what that work is was not conveyed to me. However, since there are billions of Galaxies in the Cosmos, no doubt there are untold numbers of Beings within the Zero dimensions who are actively engaged in forwarding this vast, complex existential Process.

When the three Unutterable Beings had conveyed to me – by a direct unspoken communication through the respective Lights of their Beings – the fact of their position in the Cosmos, it appeared that they had fulfilled the reason for their visit. I received the impression that I was not being favoured in any way but that they just had a duty to perform in conveying this knowledge to me. They then left, not by departing into physical space like shooting stars, but by going within the very space they had occupied in front of me. Their departure was swift.

* * * *

Over the years there had been occasional further encounters with "Mr Nothing", the Unutterable Being who had visited me during my childhood. But there came a point in my maturer years when I decided to actually invite His presence.

I wished to ask this Being to reveal to me more as to his identity. At that point in time He was the highest Zero Being I had encountered. I had not yet known our Himmonda, the eternal Supreme Being about whom I write more particularly in the following chapter. Neither at this point had I seen the Ruler of our Universe nor had benefit of yet more expansive insights which revealed the awesome vastness of the entire Cosmic Body of Creation – described in "The Brimonda" in the Cosmology of TAYOZAAN hereafter – which occurred subsequent to her visitation.

It was in about the year 1967 at my home in London, England, when I decided to seek the presence of "Mr Nothing". I wanted an answer to what at that stage of my life was a most important question. I had never before intentionally sought Him. His previous visitations had been unbidden.

I chose a day in the month of August whilst I was on holiday from work when there was the rare opportunity of some time to myself in which to quietly prepare. I worked to make the house sparklingly clean and orderly for this special occasion and having selected the room in which I should be for the event, when evening came I sat down, alone. I relaxed, and when in a clearminded, quiet state, I invited the Unutterable Being's presence.

There was instantaneous response. An Unutterable Light which I knew to be the Being I sought, appeared before me, filling the room with its special atmosphere and its deep Silence, that Silence with its all-pervasive quality of Nothingness which penetrated not only me but the very walls of the house. All was embued with that emptiness which yet at the same time is a living reality: an alivedness which both Is and Is Not.

I asked this Being simply and directly: "*Are you God? Are you the Creator?*" The Unutterable Being answered. It "spoke" with and from its Light, from its Wholeness – from the Oneness of its being – soundless, bodyless, faceless, without eyes, mouth or voice, having need of neither limbs nor organs. The centre of its Light merged with its outer and the outer edges merged with its centre. The merging and folding from all parts of the Unutterable Being's globe of Light (which, as when viewing the sun, is seen as a "disc" of Light) is of a milky silver, silkily smooth and graceful movement of utmost gentility. It is its very movement which conveys meaning. Just one movement can convey a wealth of meaning. Yet, strange and paradoxical though it may be to our human comprehension, I have to convey that when the Unutterable Light "moved", such was the experience that He both moved and He moved not. He both "spoke" and He "spoke" not. He both "Is" and He "Is Not".

Some of His communication I understood, some I did not or did not come to comprehend until much later when my own level of development had grown. But what I did understand at the time was that this Being was conveying: "*I am not God; but I am Creator and of creation*".

I was baffled by this response. I could not comprehend how, if this Being was Creator (and I assumed at that stage of my understanding that if he was Creator he must be "The" Creator) He was not also God.

The Unutterable Being conveyed so much depth in His response, giving much more than a simple reply to my questions – questions born of my human ignorance and naivety – that I was not at that time able to assimilate or benefit from all that was so richly offered.

However, having thus "spoken", the Light of the Unutterable Being's presence was suddenly seemingly absorbed into itself – and it was gone. I was left only with that extraordinary atmosphere of Nothingness and special deep Silence I had long come to associate with experience of the Zero dimensions and which, as before, continued with me for some time after His departure. I was additionally left with a great sense of wonderment; wonderment at witnessing such a totality, such Oneness of the Unutterable's Being, for it was the first time an Unutterable Light had demonstrated to me "speech" in the way of expressing communication from and with the wholeness of itself.

I was extremely perplexed by the answer I had received. I knew I could neither rest nor find peace of mind until I had resolved the conundrum of how this Unutterable Being could be Creator but not God, so I determined to invite Him again and to ask more precise questions, which I hoped would bring clear answers – bearing in mind the nature of communication from the Unutterable Dimension.

I therefore invited the Unutterable Being's presence again the following evening; and He duly appeared. This time I asked: "Did you create Adam and Eve?" "Did you create Mankind?" The answer I received was that *Creation is of He and his Kind and his Nature; but that He did not create Adam and Eve*.

This reply was again most perplexing; not only perplexing but also seemingly contradictory, for I interpreted His response as confirmation that He was Creator and I therefore assumed this was confirmation that He *and His "Kind" and His "Nature"* (whatever that might mean I had no idea at that time) created mankind here on Earth. How then could He say he did not create Adam and Eve? This did not make sense to me; and his denial that He was God, although He claimed to be Creator, caused me now even to doubt the validity of what was being conveyed to me.

Feeling, I must honestly admit, frustrated and even somewhat resentful at being left in state of yet greater confusion and turmoil of mind than before, I prepared myself to invite the Unutterable Being again on the third evening.

On this third evening I was in a highly charged state of concern and expectancy. Also this time I was in a somewhat confrontational mood. Somehow I had managed to bear the ensuing hours from the previous evening; but although I again prepared myself and silently invited the Unutterable Being's presence, this time He did not come. I waited and waited, initially with some feelings of impatience as I had come to expect He would arrive swiftly as before... but as the hours went by it was with changed emotions – now of sadness and disappointment – that I came to accept He would not on this occasion be responding to my call.

In the years that followed, I was involved in Sufism, Meditation and Yoga; but none proved to be correct, although helpful up to a point, so eventually I abandoned them all.

It was not until I had myself further developed my own Unutterable Light in the practical systems of the Philosophy of TAYOZAAN and had achieved further insight into Life that I realised the full import of what had been revealed to me by that Unutterable Being, the "Mr Empty Nothing" of my youth. I then understood that what He had conveyed to me was indeed Truth: the more complex Truth which is of deeper level of Reality.

I came to understand that the Beginning of manifest Existence results from a creative movement from within the depths of the Unutterable Dimension, that *He and his Kind* are of the *Nature* of that creative dimension but that the Unutterable Dimension is not "God". Neither is any Being of that Unutterable Nature from which Creation (the creative Process of manifest Existence) emanates, "God".

The understanding conveyed invalidates the "God" of the Bible or the "God" of the Koran.

The answer conveyed by the Unutterable Light that neither He nor His Kind nor his Nature created Adam and Eve was also eventually understood: no such beings having existed. The Biblical story is but a story; in fact the story is a lie.

* * * *

The Unutterable level of Being is an IS NOT state, so described as it is a dimension beyond all experience known to our ordinary senses in this finite dimension of *Existence*. It is beyond the confines of the laws of physical Existence. It is a state beyond any adequate description in words, it is beyond the imagination and it cannot be reached or induced by the use of drugs or auto suggestion. It is also beyond the level of our ordinary dream world but if they so choose, Beings of the Zero worlds can enter our dream state.

The Unutterable Dimension is of Light unlike any light of this gross manifest world; and its Light has quality. For want of language which can truly describe the "positive" elements of its quality I can only express it in such words as Beauteous Intelligence irradiating Loving Gratitude. It is Power; it is Force. It is Eternal by nature.

When man is sufficiently developed he also is of this eternal Zero quality and nature even whilst still in physical form here in manifest Existence.

The achieving of the Unutterable state, whilst truly extra-ordinary from the viewpoint of this manifest dimension, is in fact very "ordinary" from higher viewpoint because it is normal to that dimension. It is the "common" state of those who have achieved the first level of eternal Zero development. There are, therefore, countless numbers of Unutterable Beings within creation – as we will all eventually come to know for ourselves, for every human being is possessed of its Zero roots and potential and the Unutterable Light of each of us is in its inexorable process of evolution.

However, the Unutterable Dimension is not only the source of high quality. It being the zone of creativity, it is also the source of *imperfection.*

THE HIMMONDA

It has been stated, and long believed, that one cannot go beyond the level of the **Unutterable**, the “Brahman” of Aryan Hinduism.

The Unutterable, that unseen cause of the manifest World of Creation has, understandably, been considered “God”, the Highest of the Highest, beyond which or beyond whom one cannot go. And indeed, when first experiencing the awe inspiring other-worldly quality of a Being of the Unutterable Dimension, one would not expect to find nor therefore look for anything beyond that rarified, timeless state. But I came to be aware of something of indefinable “substance” yet further within the depths of the Unutterable Light: a Light of yet more intense Zeroness, of yet more rarified “Nothingness” within the depths of the Unutterable Light. I gradually came to connect with this deeper dimensional quality, to an ever increasing extent as my own Unutterable Light matured.

This matured Unutterable depth is of the nature and substance of an Eternal reality which TAYOZAAN has named the **Non Existent Dimension**. Although a *totally* **IS NOT** “Zero” state from the finite existential viewpoint, the Non Existent Dimension is the truly **IS** state within the depth of the Unutterable IS NOT Zeroness. Non Existence is a completely infinite, eternal dimension.

When a human being has developed his or her Unutterable Light into a Self of Non Existent dimensional quality, that Self is of **Himmond** level. There are countless numbers of Beings within the physical Cosmos and within the Zero Cosmos who are at variously different levels of internal/eternal development; and there are untold numbers of Beings who have attained Himmond status.

More rare, however, is the Himmond whose Non Existent depth achieves such maturity that its Blessing (an act of emission of supreme Love and Gratitude) towards the manifest World produces a further thrust of creational activity into the physical Cosmos. TAYOZAAN has named a Being of such level of development and capability a **Himmonda**. This kind of Blessing of a Being of such quality and potency may be deemed an act of cosmic procreation.

A Himmonda is a truly Supreme Eternal Being. *There are millions of Himmondas* but it is nevertheless a relatively rare and special achievement to reach this level of Completion.

Our Himmonda – the Creator of this section of the cosmos in which lies our own Universe – has communicated from His Light of Non Existent dimensional Being. That Light, which is unlike the nature of anything one may encounter in this manifest world, is of yet different quality and of much greater brilliance than that of the Unutterable Light. It is an immensely concentrated pale blue brilliance with its own vibrational quality: a Light which is experienced as a composite of qualities. Although its "hallmark", its distinguishing Non Existent quality or "atmosphere", is likewise a "Nothingness", its Zeroness is uniquely its own.

Although, as with the Unutterable Light, it is a "*Living* Zeroness", it has its own uniquely qualitied ITNESS or "personality": one of immensely more rarified depth than that of the Unutterable level, irradiating Love and

Wisdom of a quality, depth and intensity special to its own nature.

I later came to appreciate that Beings of such high level of development do not necessarily show their Light. They can do so or be invisible at will.

* * * *

My experiences of our Himmonda began when I had been searching the internal dimensional worlds within my own depths questing further knowledge. I was hungry for greater understanding of this mysterious life. As I searched I became aware of a distant Light, a Light which gave the impression of journeying towards me from afar within internal space. I kept my attention upon this Light, which gradually drew yet closer...but then the experience ended. However I connected this experience with my internal searching and was happy to be reaping some tangible result.

Soon afterwards I sought this Light again and it duly appeared. With the viewing was the knowledge that it was the same Light, the same Being, as had previously made itself known to me.

It proved necessary to look for this Being a third time before it became close enough to enable actual communication between us.

On the first occasion when I saw the Himmonda's Light I had seen that He was too far away, like some distant star – alone in His dimensional realm. In observing His coming I saw His approach to be seemingly in three stages, as if He had been as it were three sections of distance away from me. At greatest distance His Light appeared reddish pink in colour but as He drew nearer

His Light changed until it gradually became the pale blue-ish hue I have come to associate with His Light.

Before I came to understand that this Light was our Himmonda, I was wanting to know more of this Being. In effect I was wishing to investigate Him for my previous experiences had made me cautious. I did not want to be misled by Life's dark opposition. I was therefore wary lest this be some deception of Anti Life Force nature.

However, when the Himmonda finally arrived it was apparent that He knew exactly what was in my mind and He immediately "spoke"... from and *with* his Light, that is from and with the wholeness of His Being. With my seeing of this Light of Non Existent quality came the knowledge of who this Supreme Himmonda Being was: that He was the cause of and the Being responsible for our own Mahaverse: that vast cosmic section (composed of billions of Universes) within the total body of manifest Existence, in which our own Universe has its place.

Communication from a Being of Himmonda level is more swift, intense and concentrated and therefore much more difficult to comprehend than has been my experience of Beings of the Unutterable dimensional level. Communication is similarly from and with the Light of its entire Being, without use or need of language or sound; but with an Unutterable Light the phenomenon is of a more simple nature and is therefore more easy to understand.

The Himmonda's Light was also distinctly different; not of the milky, self luminous transparency of a Being of Unutterable dimensional level. The Light of a Being of Non Existent Zeroness is likewise self luminous and transparent but its self luminosity is of the most intense (yet non dazzling) *brilliance*, its transparency being sheenily glassy. Its brilliance has a silvery, mirrorlike quality.

Due to the intensity – the sheer *purity* of the simplicity of its unified state – and the immediacy of transmission caused by the speed of this Being's communication, I found it most difficult to comprehend what was being conveyed, for although it is a potent form of direct communication to another's knowing intelligence, one needs to be of sufficiently advanced level oneself to be adequately receptive. However, just to experience His presence and view the Light of this Being was in itself invaluable. I saw that as His Light projected itself in sharply swift, electronic like emissions of communication, so at the very same time it silkily folded those emissions back into itself – *but yet it did not move*. It retained its supremely qualitied *stillness*. Even when intensely active, such a Being remains complete and poised in the perfection of itself.

I now know that the Zero Light of a Being of wholly Non Existent nature is the substance of Life itself. And I saw the Himmonda's "speech" to be movement of the wholeness of His own Life substance. Therefore His "speech" was sharply definite, it being the totality of Himself in action; yet with that sharp immediacy of expression was conveyed feeling and depth – and an intrinsic quality of utmost gentleness.

* * * *

There have been further occasions when the Himmonda has appeared to me, without my having sought Him. He has come when some deep question has been on my mind. On one such occasion I just wished to know more of Him and He came, this time revealing Himself not as a Light of Non Existent nature but showing Himself within the Stabilising Dimension in the form in which He had experienced His final incarnation in human flesh.

Where the Himmonda had existed within the Cosmos during his physical incarnations I do not know but He showed that He had been in male form in His last human incarnation and that His face had borne Mongolian-type features. Or perhaps it is more accurate to say His countenance was similar to that of the Mongolian/Chinese/Japanese type grouping of people as we know them here on this planet. As I viewed Him His features were altering in a fast flowing succession of changes. Many faces were shown, all with similar type features, and I understood He was conveying to me that He had lived many lives in a certain kind of human grouping.

The Himmonda also came to me on an occasion when I was ill. He again came within the Stabilising Dimension, projecting Himself in human form and although the form was not recognisable from the previous images he had shown, I knew from the special "atmosphere" of His "Presence" that it was He.

I was lying in bed when He came. He arrived during the small hours of the morning before dawn; and He proferred me honey in a stainless steel spoon. It was a gesture of compassion and concern; and although I was not healed, I was immensely grateful for and comforted by the act.

It may sound strange that the Himmonda offered me honey in a stainless steel spoon, but the Stabilising Dimension is that which bridges our physical world with the Zero worlds. It was a symbolic act; one of sincere simplicity – and for me much more telling and valuable than if I had been proferred honey from the internal worlds in a silver or golden spoon.

The term "impossibility" which applies to all stages of Existence does not apply to the Unutterable or Non Existent dimensions. A different "reality" applies to the Zero dimensions. Therefore although a Being of Himmonda stature is not everywhere, He can be anywhere. Also, whilst He is of immense power, that power is not necessarily displayed.

I have come to understand that our Himmonda does not generally interfere with the process of the natural Law of Life. It is possible He may intervene from time to time. I have yet to understand more as to the work of these higher dimensional Beings. No doubt they have important roles and responsibilities but exactly what form their work takes I do not yet know.

* * * *

The main knowledge derived from encounters with this Himmonda has been that He is the Being whose Blessing, whose thrust of creativity, occasioned the creation of this particular section of the vast Cosmos in which our own Universe has its place; this relatively small section alone being composed of millions of Universes.

Further to this understanding has come the dramatic confirmation that His creative achievement (awesomely extraordinary though it may appear to we mortals at this stage of our evolution) is an achievement which is in fact within the range of possibilities open to other humans who evolve themselves to similar stage of Completion; for Himmondas have themselves arisen from the evolutionary Process of Life. Our own Himmonda was Himself once mortal: a human being who developed His own "Seed" of Existence, who refined the Zeroness of the Light of His own Life. He Himself therefore originated from a Beginning as have we all. He has matured Himself to such point of Completion that He has become the cause of a further Beginning. And He is but one of countless numbers of other Creators.

It is therefore not true to speak of there being only one Creator. But I now understand that such thrusts of creativity which produce the phenomenon of physical manifestation always involve the Unutterable dimension – that "Brahman" Zero level of creativity – which, from within the depth of the Stabilising dimension, links the infinite Zero Worlds with the finite Physical Worlds of Existence.

A further, profoundly important directive from our Himmonda – which He emphasised to point of severity - was that we should not beg or ask Him for help; nor should we worship Him. I came to clearly understand this longheld attitude and behaviour to have been born out of ignorance; and that such stance and action is badly misguided for it not only interferes with but it actually hinders our development.

As to the begging stance of prayer, the Himmonda emphasised with force that we must have confidence in the depth of our own intelligent sincerity and make our own efforts. I came to see quite clearly that to beseech in prayer drains and weakens our Light which we should instead be working to strengthen and to ennoble with its own qualities and power. Prayer is a truly wrong, misguided action which has plagued humanity for millenia.

As to worship, I similarly came clearly to understand just how unnecessary (how quite stupid in fact) it is to praise the higher Zero Beings. They have no need whatsoever for our worship or obeisance. From our human standpoint, again it is a wasteful, unproductive action. All that is necessary is for us to acknowledge – with gratitude and respect – the fact of their higher dimensional reality and to make sincere endeavour to reach their position... or even advance further.

* * * *

Despite the Himmonda's strict injunction that we should not ask for help, I did nevertheless seek Him again at a time when I was very troubled. It was when my first book "TAYOZAAN - The Fourth Beginning" was about to be printed. In that book (my first exposition of the philosophy of TAYOZAAN) I had revealed a disturbing discovery – which was that a human being's thoughts inevitably degenerate into the Anti Life force of opposition, albeit of varying types and intensity according to the strength of the thought and the quality of feeling accompanying the thought.

This is probably a truth known to the Aryan Hindus and at least sensed by other philosophical disciplines as they speak of the need to "still" the mind from thinking. I know it is no answer to try to stop the mind from working and I also know that to endeavour to "still" the mind is an unhealthy practice which only weakens this most precious instrument. I therefore feared that by speaking of my discovery that thought produces Anti Life Force it would have the effect of convincing people they do indeed need to still their thinking processes as is taught by some spiritual disciplines. I wanted to know whether this statement should be omitted from my book.

The Himmonda was swift to respond. His response was in effect a harsh reprimand. His demeanour was of chiding anger at my weakness. His previous statement was repeated. His Light conveyed: "*Do not ever ask for help. Do what you have to do*". And the question was not answered.

This was a most salutary lesson which struck deep and indelibly. I was in fact shocked by the anger within the force of His response and from that point onwards I have never asked for help. I determined thereafter always to speak the truth where necessary and to stand my ground fearlessly.

I felt then and continue to feel immense gratitude towards the Himmonda for his wisdom. My gratitude deepened as that wisdom became ever more clearly understood with the passage of time. I indeed thank Him for being my greatest and truest Friend.

So many times have I remembered that lesson, with continuing gratitude for the enormous advances reaped from having the courage to stand by my own convictions; to stand in the confidence of what has become my own knowledge of truth. One reaps by making one's own striving efforts. The effort has to be self motivated and self achieved regardless of the density of the darkness which may face us or lie ahead of us.

* * * *

At one point I strongly desired to know more of this great Being, our Himmonda. The question in my mind was whether He was alone in His eternal sphere. I had only seen Him and I wondered whether He was with other Beings of similar level of Completion. As a human being the thought of his possible aloneness in the vastness of Reality concerned me. From my own point of view such a destiny would be frighteningly lacking.

On this occasion, in contemplative state and quietly alone, I observed a grouping of some thirty Lights, like stars in a formation in the firmament – but this was vision not of finite matter but of the supra physical realm within the Zero dimensions. With the seeing was the knowledge that these Lights were a grouping of Himmondas. As they were grouped the Lights were in the formation of a figure nine but a nine with as it were a curved tail. However, the loop or circle of the letter nine was sideways on to my vision, as one would see the rim of a cup placed before one; and in a position in the centre of the rim closest to my view was our Himmonda.

All the Lights of the Himmondas in that cluster, or formation, were of similar brilliance. They were all Beings of the same nature yet they each retained their own individuality; and it was clear to me which Light was our own Himmonda.

On the occasion of this viewing I further wanted to know whether this was the only such grouping of Himmondas – and then I saw that afar off were other formations of Himmondas with distances between each grouping. Some clusters of Himmondas were larger than others. From what I could observe, there are many, many such assemblies of Himmonda Beings stretching into infinity.

I was able to make contact as far as the group just beyond that of our own Himmonda. This formation of Himmondas showed themselves to be aware of me, conveying a "smiling" loving interest. In fact they appeared very glad to be knowing and making contact with me.

I observed with great interest, and sense of comfort, that the Himmondas have not lost their individuality in achievement of Supreme Oneness of Being.

* * * *

Our Himmonda came from a section of the Cosmos which had been created by its own Himmonda. And there are millions of other Himmondas who have similarly been the cause of and who are responsible for their own sections of the Cosmos. This is the self replicating process occurring within the total body of the Cosmos. The total Body of Existence has been named by TAYOZAAN the **Brimonda**.

However, although millions of acts of cosmic creativity into this vast physical Brimonda are occurring, in relation to the innumerable Beings who reach Himmond level, the achieving of *Himmonda* status is still a very special and rare occurrence.

So we see that there is no end to the flow of creation. There is no end to Beginnings in the vast spectrum of Existence; nor is there any end to the flow of Creation's evolutionary movement towards maturation on the long road to Life's final Completion.

Our Himmonda, the Supreme Being of this our own section of the Cosmos, functions throughout the dimensions. He does not need our praise or obeisance, nor is such outpouring required of us as a means of maturing our Light. On the contrary, such wastage of our energies disables and thwarts our progress, drugging our intelligence so that we are blinded from discerning what is in fact correct internal action.

Our Himmonda only requires for us our eventual perfection, for each Being to stand supreme in its own right in Oneness with all Creation, as does He.

We need to be grateful towards Life. We need to work for our own perfection – and to help others. To aim for the very nature of the Being of each of us to be of quality of Love, Gratitude and Compassion in strength of Wisdom is a glorious desire. It is also an achievable goal.

The Supreme Beings require nothing of us but that we achieve the goal of Life. We are free to aspire to that goal, the highest of Life's possibilities. That goal is the goal of TAYOZAAN which is to attain HIMMZAANON Completion in the Timeless Zeroness of ZAHTAUM; a state of Being beyond even that of the Himmondas.

THE COSMOLOGY OF TAYOZAAN

By way of simple illustration of what is meant when I speak of the various *dimensions* of Life, visualise if you will a line before your mental gaze – a perpendicular line – to the left of which conceptualise the vast *external* world, the dimension of **Physical Existence**, composed as it is of *billions* of Universes. Physical Existence, the world of matter, includes all fleshly bodily forms. To the right of this imaginary line, direct your attention *internally* to the Mind world within you. Mind is of the "spiritual" or **Zero Worlds** of a subtler, invisible nature, belonging to an internal reality beyond that of physical existence. Let your Mind observe itself. Understand that within the depths of your Mind is the Light of the very *Life* which you are. Also understand that your essential Self: the Light of Life within you, together with your supraphysical organ of Mind, are the gateway to ever subtler depths of reality. These internal dimensional depths of reality are called the "Zero" Worlds because their nature conveys atmosphere of an extraordinary "Nothingness". Experience of them is of a totally different quality to anything known to our ordinary physical senses in this manifest existence. What follows is a Vision of Life resulting from experiences garnered over long course of time: observations – of this gargantuan gross Cosmos of physical existence and of the depthful internal/eternal Zero dimensions from which the physical Cosmos arose – viewed from the depths of my own internal dimensional nature. All dimensions – the Physical Worlds and the Zero Worlds – together comprise one Reality: the Oneness, the living Allness of Life.

CREATION

In some versions of the biblical Old Testament the Book of Genesis states: "In the Beginning was the Word" and "the Word was God". But related here is a perception of Creation observed from the vision of reality which is TAYOZAAN.

TAYOZAAN is a viewpoint of the way things are in both human and cosmic terms. In the microscopic can be seen reflection of the greater, macroscopic reality. Life: Existence and Non Existence, is a great multi-layered *Process*. There is intelligence, there are laws affecting and maintaining this Process. There are Truths which are seen to apply equally throughout the various dimensional levels – in grosser or subtler form, dependant upon the level being observed. But it is also seen that there is a different perspective of Truth from each dimensional level. The great Process functions within all dimensional levels and is interconnected but each dimension is of its own distinctive quality. Each dimension, each internal/eternal depth, has its own ITNESS, its own uniquely qualitied nature of Zeroness.

Viewing the position in human terms, the "Word" is not at the commencement of creativity. Before the expression of the Word is Thought. The creation of Thought is inspired from the complex depth of consciousness which is our essential Self. Our "Self" is our very *Life* together with its content of experience, for we carry with our Life force an essence of experience garnered in a long process of evolution. It is that depth of our Being which is the precursor to Thought. It is that depth of *Self* which is the motivator and energiser of Thought.

Our "Self", in the language of the philosophy of TAYOZAAN, is the *Seed of Existence* within us. The

Seed of Existence is also referred to as the *Light* within us – for it is in fact seen (with internal vision) to be a disc of Light. Actually it is a globe of Light but it appears as a disc, just as does the sun or moon to our vision. That Light of our Selfhood – or Seed of Existence within us – is, as I have said, our Life force together with our content of experience and is therefore what we essentially are. What we are is based on the level of evolution (in its holistic sense) which each of us may have reached at any given point in time and constitutes the real and true Self of our individuality.

Our own individual Seed of Existence, founded as it is on its own creative depth, is that which motivates Mind. Mind is the supra physical organ which bridges our internal and external dimensional worlds. Mind is where thought and intelligence arise and where concepts are born. Mind – that invisible organ of internal dimensional nature – is stimulated/energised by the creative movements of our Light. It is therefore motivated from our essential Self. Movements of Mind in turn motivate and energise our physical brains. Impulses from the brain activate the body – and voice – to expression. And so is produced the manifest "word". This is the reality in human terms.

Similarly, in cosmic terms, the Beginning of manifest Life was (and is) an expression emanating from yet deeper dimensional depths. Astronomers refer to the "Big Bang" as being the Beginning of the Cosmos; but the manifest, physical Cosmos of Matter has been seen to result from creative movement generating from an *eternal* dimension: from the eternal Third level of Beginning. This creative thrust into the existential dimension results from a descending chain of creative impulses through the eternal depths, commencing from the nature of the ITNESS of Primary Zeroness which is seen to be the First Beginning, the initial source of all Life. The Third level of Beginning – the level of creativity from which manifest life commenced – is what is termed "Brahman" in Aryan Hinduism. TAYOZAAN has named this creative level of Third Beginning the "**UNUTTERABLE**" Dimension.

The Unutterable Dimension is of the **IS NOT** eternal nature, being of a quite different level of reality from that of matter. However complex and sophisticated manifest physical existence may become, it still remains within and of the external world of matter, connected though it be with its supra physical depths.

The *Unutterable* is so named because it cannot really be described. There is no vocabulary to adequately describe it for it cannot be compared to anything known to our ordinary existential experience. It is of a completely different quality. For want of adequate language, TAYOZAAN expresses the nature of that quality as "Zeroness", for it is a complete "Nothingness". That "Nothingness" is not an "emptiness" nor is it a "vacuum", both of which words are descriptive of conditions relating to this physical dimension. Its extraordinary quality, whilst we have the capacity to experience it, is totally beyond anything known to our physical senses.

That which bridges the Unutterable and the physical dimensions is termed by TAYOZAAN the "**STABILISING**" Dimension. This is more generally known as the "spiritual" dimension – which much of humankind has for millenia accepted, or at least believed, to form a subtler part of the reality of this physical existence. In fact all physical matter has within it this subtler, internal counterpart. It is as it were the blueprint of the outer physical form. More is said of this dimensional reality elsewhere in this book but it should be clarified here that Mind is of the "spiritual" level of this Stabilising dimension. The invisible organ of Mind is our active link, our conscious connection between the outer physical, sensory world and the Unutterable and yet deeper internal dimensions.

A movement of creation from the Unutterable level emanates from its own depths. The Unutterable Dimension is activated from the yet deeper Zeroness of what TAYOZAAN terms the "**NON EXISTENT**" Dimension which is within the depth of the Unutterable Dimension. Non Existence was (and is) before Existence.

The Non Existent Dimension is that eternal depth which is the Second level of Beginning in the descending chain of creative thrust from primary source of First Beginning. The Non Existent Dimension is a truly **IS** state in the quality of its own eternal infinite nature and is itself moved from within its own depths. It is moved from the Zeroness, from the **ITNESS of First Beginning**.

The First Beginning, the commencing source or nature, the **Eternal ITNESS**, never ceases. Its eternal order or nature is in constant state of Beginning which, in its own incomprehensible timescale, takes a very long while to *Be*. That Primordial ITNESS is essentially very basic and crude. It has been viewed – from level of my own Non Existent dimensional Being – as a living Black Mass, a mass so black I could not (on that particular viewing) see its movement; but with the seeing was the knowledge that it moves. I was also conscious of its own ITNESS "personality" of primordial Zeroness.

On a subsequent witnessing of this eternal Zeroness of First Beginning I saw the movement of the Black Mass.

It was making inward swirling movements as though gathering itself towards itself. These spinning, inward turning motions appeared to be achieving a "clumping" effect within its mass. It was also creating a defined, extraordinarily dense or "hard", exterior to the mass. This "denseness", this "hardness" was a denseness and hardness of its own substance or nature. It was apparent that its movements were generating a tremendous force within itself. It was later seen to have assumed a contour, a shape which I would liken to that of the round style of beehive used in olden days. Its shape gradually changed until it became akin to that of an old fashioned wooden barrel. Parts of the extremity of the massed shape were smooth, some parts were lumpily rough like wooden staving around a bulbous barrel.

Another viewing showed the barrel-shaped Black Mass silently bursting or "exploding" (there was no sound, only an inner viewing). The happening was very violent. I saw a straight greenish/blue column of light generate horizontally across the centre of the Black Mass. With the seeing was the knowledge that the generating of this column of light had been the cause of the bursting explosion. This column of Light I have named the "Afcol".

On another viewing I saw this column of Light, the Afcol, move from the horizontal to the perpendicular position and then begin complex swift motions, crisscrossing movements of light, the initially straight column of Light thereby changing into a myriad small lights. Gathering, spinning or circular movements gradually formed these fragmented lights into a global, bulbous shape until it became a moving mass of Light. A breathing movement seemed to unite the whole global mass – the myriad mass of lights – into a vivified ITNESS thereby producing its own Time and Space. Its own Time and Space is of its own nature, not as of the nature of the Time and Space of the existential, manifest world.

This I knew to be the commencing process towards but prior to the Beginning of the manifest physical world of matter. I do not know how many times this phenomenon of gathering, the generating of immense force and explosive bursting occurs within the deep Zero dimensions before point of creation of physical matter is reached.

* * * *

All possibility lies within the very First Beginning. It is the Architect of Architects; the Creator of Creators. It is an EVER IS state, an eternally permanent Presence. Yet in the First Beginning there is no word, there is no thought, there is no up nor down, no right nor wrong, no direction as such – just a growing expansion of Itself. There is no I nor you, only Thatness: **ITNESS**. There is no intelligence, knowledge or wisdom. It asks no question nor can it answer any. The First Beginning does not know what it is. It does not know Itself. The Beginning of Beginnings is blanketed in Silence. It moves. And it grows. Its action, its movement is Creation. The basic Zero nature of First Beginning is to **BE** and to **MOVE**. This originating Zeroness is Oneness which can never cease to Be; and nothing of the entirety of all that Is and Is Not can be separated from that Oneness. Its nature of Oneness and perpetual movement of creativity in action of Becoming is reflected throughout all the dimensional levels which constitute the Allness of Life. Primary Zero ITNESS is Brahman's nature. Inherent in its nature of Zeroness/Oneness and Movement/Creation is Life/Anti-Life, Dream/Illusion and Reality/Mystery.

Knowledge of the First Beginning comes from an internally developed Being. No such knowledge was or is in the First Beginning Itself but it is nevertheless the Eternal Architect of Architects, the Commencement from deepest depth in a never ceasing chain of Beginnings. When we, who in fact arose from **before** the beginning of existential Time from the Timeless Nature of First Beginning, have matured ourselves sufficiently into "substance" of the eternal depths, then that matured, Completed Being which we will have become, will know Itself. It will know Itself as matured First Beginning. It will then know the nature of First Beginning for the matured Life contributes to and itself produces the depth of the Zero ITNESS of First Beginning, the primary source and fount of all possibilities; but that Completed Being will not know the totality of Itself until the "End" has been fully achieved.

That basic Zero ITNESS of First Beginning we each of us can even now identify with. We can sense it applies to our own essential Self beyond the accumulated persona we have become. Within our depth of depths, you and I just ARE.

* * * *

Movement from the Non Existent depths therefore activates the Unutterable dimensional level and whenever there is movement from the Unutterable dimension there is manifestation: a further creational beginning within the world of physical matter.

I have observed such a movement from the Unutterable Dimension. On this occasion I saw a vast quantity and intensity of Light: Light which I knew to be of the Unutterable nature. The vibrational quality of

Unutterable nature is one of supreme Love... Loving Gratitude. It also conveys its Power and Force. Creative movement from the Unutterable Dimension is similar to that of the Afcol, the column of Light seen in the movement from First Beginning. A similar column of Light was seen to move from the horizontal downward to the perpendicular and then commence crisscrossing and revolving, inward gathering actions of its myriad fragmented particles of Light; movements of great speed and complexity. It moved thus, condensing itself to itself, until it assumed a global, bulbous shape of luminous activity. The luminosity continued to absorb itself towards its centre – the knowledge being that this inward movement of absorption took place over a vast period of existential Time. In the long process of absorption its centre gradually contracted, darkening to a dense black substance, the gathering actions generating tremendous force within itself, similar in pattern to that previously observed within the Black Mass of First Beginning; but on this occasion, when the Black Mass burst forth, fragmenting its substance in a gigantic (yet for me silent) explosion, I knew this action of creativity from level of the Unutterable Dimension to be the beginning of Matter, the beginning of manifestation within the dimension of the physical World ... a World which is “Perfect Imperfection”...so called as there is inherent Imperfection within Existence, but this Imperfection has purpose, it being a necessary forcefield of opposition to enable us to achieve ultimate Perfection.

Similar processes – of relentless movement in the rotating, gathering and contracting of matter substance, the generating of energy and explosive occurrences – have continued, thus producing the vast multitude of cosmic formations within space which are observable in this manifest dimension of the Physical Worlds.

Space is also Life – the most primitive form of Life – more primeval than Matter. Space cannot be damaged. Space also moves within space, for there are different kinds of space. Although not a phenomenon relative to this physical level, in the reality of the Stabilising or "spiritual" dimension, Space is seen to be in shapes of squares and oblongs which have flat "faces" and there is communication between the different portions of space. These different portions of Space "chatter" to one another with sound; a sound like the distorted human voice when a recording is played at too high a speed. They are seen to be primitively "happy" and "carefree" in their realm of existence. Space was (and is) the female element. The substance of the condensed Black Mass – the commencing Matter of physical dimensional nature – was (and is) male element and is Time.

When a creational surge from the supra physical dimensions reaches level of manifestation, the life vibration slows into grosser vibration as it proceeds further from source. Gross matter is affected and "moved" by rigorous, complex processes of evolution involving eons of Time. Creativity of various kinds proceeds unceasingly at all levels. Within the vast framework of exchanges and interactions of Cosmic energies, procreation proceeds unceasingly within Existence together with an extraordinarily complex structure of subcreational and supreme creational activity.

"Subcreation" and "supreme creation" arise from the unceasing activity of the Light of Life within manifest forms. A never ceasing field of creativity is at work in the interplay of intelligence, emotion and physical action. This form of creativity is capable of producing either grosser substance of energy – which may be termed of "*sub*human" nature – or the qualities of energy generated and our actions can create substance of higher dimensional level. What is produced depends upon the level of Being at work, its motivation and quality of accomplishment.

The complex and diverse range of activity and interaction occurring at all levels and within all aspects of manifestation combine to produce the wondrous and wide diversity of life which constitutes Existence.

The primordial Life element thus undergoes cycles of evolutionary maturation – over unimaginable eons of Time. From the most elemental state of Matter within initially the most primitive of environments there eventually arise more and more complex and sophisticated conditions and forms of life. And the process still continues. We are aware that our own planet at present hosts plant, animal and human life forms some of which may be considered quite advanced in evolutionary terms...but there is a very long way yet to go.

* * * *

The Life element within Matter – of nature of the Unutterable Dimension – is within the multitudinous diversity of manifest forms. This Life element, our Unutterable Light, passing through numerous existences in various forms in a maturing process of evolution, involves us in countless births and deaths. Death is a prerequisite to there being Birth into a new condition of existence. Life itself can never be destroyed. It can only change its form and state. Life originated from the Primary Zeroness of First Beginning: the indestructible Oneness of Reality. And the Zero nature of each of us is of and connected with that First Beginning.

We need to experience many existences at each level of maturation in many kinds of manifest form. We arrive here in this present incarnation in human form. We arrive as an individualised particle of Life which is at its current level of evolution having proceeded from a long, long past. Therefore, although we come into the world as a baby, the *Life* of that infant is billions of years old. In fact we originated before physical Time was.

This process of evolution gradually produces an essence of increasingly intelligent consciousness belonging to the Unutterable Light within each life form. The continuing experiencing of such intelligent consciousness eventually produces an ever increasing awareness and maturity of Being. We cannot escape being moulded by our experiences whilst living in this finite existence. We are subjected during the course of many incarnations to Life's laws, to its processes of nurture, destruction and harmonising balance. Some may learn more quickly and may therefore mature faster than others but eventually, inevitably, a concentrated essence of Being is produced. And so arises individuality. But that matured Light, which has developed "individuality", is never separate from the rest of manifest existence neither is it separate from the supraphysical reality of the Unutterable and Non Existent dimensions – any more than it can ever be divorced from its originating source of Primary First Beginning. *Our individual essence, the Light which is our Life, is always of all Life and all Life is of it.*

* * * *

It can therefore be comprehended that evolutionary processes within physical Existence – the evolution of initially primitive Matter within existential time and space – eventually produce sophisticated life forms which become possessed of an increasingly matured spark of the essential Unutterable Light; increasing maturity bringing in its train an increasingly heightened sense of individuality. By the time we have reached animal level, and certainly by the time our Life has achieved human form, the initial spark of Unutterable Light within us has achieved a fair degree of maturity. That *Light,* that Seed of Existence within us – whatever its stage of maturity or development may be at any given point in time – *is what we **are***. It is our *Life*. It constitutes our essential and *true Self*, or that which can be said to be our *current identity*. For that identity, that which we truly are, changes with maturity.

It must be emphasised that *maturity is not in or with the Beginning of Creation.* Only the potential is there. Maturity is produced, built and earned through long process of evolution. We therefore cannot claim to be what we have not yet achieved. We are that which we have become at any given point in time. But all possibility still lies within our common heritage and belongs to the potential destiny of each and every one of us.

When our eyes are opened, our reason for being, our main work and purpose begins to be understood. When we acknowledge the need to develop our Light, the Seed of Existence within us, we then consciously connect with the innate motivating force within all Life. We are then set to co-operate with Life's never ceasing creativity in its hunger and urge to Be. We then co-operate with its unstoppable, relentless movement towards total Completion.

We need to achieve an intensity of depth and quality of our Unutterable Light, working towards the eventual attainment of a fully matured Self of the Unutterable eternal nature. Whilst doing so, there begins to take place internal penetration into the Non Existent dimension. A momentum is set in train which produces a natural further progression of internal movement. And when a level of awareness, understanding and co-operation is reached, passage into these higher, eternal dimensions can be ever more intentionally and intelligently forged. Once we consciously agree to assist the process, with right action our progress is greatly enhanced and significantly speeded up.

One has to *build* one's eternal Self. It has to be *earned.* It results from the dedication of unceasing, correct effort. It also requires one's subtly intense, intelligent sincerity. One has to be severely honest with oneself. It is necessary to recognise and to prune away all that which is false within us, cleansing from our Light and Mind all the superfluous and damaging "baggage" which hinders our transformation – our transmutation – into yet more refined quality of Zeroness. It is a great Coming to BE. A progressively maturing Unutterable Self eventually builds within the depths of its substance a Selfhood of Non Existent dimensional nature. One then has a Being of eternal substance which can continue within the eternal dimensions after death of the physical body. No longer is there then further need to be reincarnated into the existential world.

When an individual has matured his or her Unutterable depth into the nature of Non Existent Selfhood, that Being has reached level of a Himmond. A **Himmond** is an eternally developed Being who has potential to become a Himmonda but is not yet of that level of creative power. There are untold numbers of Himmonds within the Zero Worlds. An **Himmonda** is a Completed Being who has fully developed his Non Existent Self and whose own Blessing projects creative force similar in nature and action to that occurring from the primary Zeroness of First Beginning thus eventually causing a new thrust of creativity from the Unutterable dimensional level of Third Beginning. Himmondas are therefore the cause of further manifestations into the physical world of matter. Such a new beginning of creation from the Completed Being of an Himmonda, who has achieved maturity within the manifest level of Third Beginning, is a *Fourth Beginning*. Our own **Mahaverse** - which is but one section of the total Body of Existence and which is itself composed of millions of Universes (including our own Universe) – is such a Fourth Beginning. Our Mahaverse, that section of the entire Body of Existence in which we find ourselves, was caused by and is the responsibility of our own Himmonda.

Our own Himmonda, by virtue of such creative achievement, is a Supreme Being. Although it is a rare achievement to reach the status of a Supreme Being, there are vast numbers of other Himmondas, other Supreme Beings who have similarly been the cause of and who are responsible for numerous other sections of the total Body of Existence.

That total Body of manifest Existence, is named in the philosophy of TAYOZAAN our "**Brimonda**". The composition of the Brimonda is more particularly described in the following chapter.

* * * *

Therefore in addition to manifest Existence originating from a descending chain of creative movement from the Primary Zeroness of First Beginning, yet further and similar acts of what may be termed "cosmic procreation" result from the Blessings of Supreme Beings. As has been mentioned above, such further acts of creation from the qualitied force of the Light of Supreme Beings TAYOZAAN has named "Fourth" Beginnings. Fourth Beginnings result from the matured Life Force. There are untold numhers of such new creations.

The Brimonda – the entire manifest body of physical existence – is continuing to grow. The Brimonda is continuing to expand with new creations resulting from cosmic procreational surges of activity from Himmondas. At the same time the content of this gargantuan, ever expanding Brimonda is progressively maturing. This maturing and growth is taking place at all dimensional levels. Whilst there is evolution within the "gross" physical dimension, simultaneously there is evolution taking place within the internal, eternal Zero dimensional depths of Life.

It is therefore the Brimonda which produces its gem; and eventually it is the gem which produces the Brimonda.

It follows that there is potential possibility for you and I, as maturing Beings within the Brimonda, to likewise eventually create substance of Life as has the Being – the Himmonda – who created the Fourth Beginning from which we have arisen... that is when and if we achieve similar level of Completion.

Purposeful movement, real creative achievement, is therefore twofold: an epic cycle of maturing and growth which, seen from our human existential perspective, is seemingly in two opposite directions, one direction being an external growth and maturing into the world of matter and the other being an internal growth and maturing into the Zero Worlds. But in fact all levels are connected and at Zero depth are seen to comprise one Total Reality. The cyclic process commences with movement of the Primary Zero ITNESS of First Beginning as described above. By means of manifest Existence, Life progressively evolves to the point when it produces further Life not merely by duplicating its form procreationally but by producing Zero qualitied "substance" to power the emergence of new Creation.

Life supports Itself. *Life in effect is its own meal.* And Life creates Life.

Eventually that emanation from First Beginning develops itself into its total-dimensional Selfhood. This is achieved through the maturing of individualised particles of that initial Life Force of Primary Zeroness. We, that is we human beings, are such individualised life particles of that Primary Zero ITNESS who are in midst of that long, purposeful, maturing Process. We can therefore now see the reason for our journey.

A totally matured Supreme Being within the Cosmos is one who has reached *ZAHTAUM* level of Completion. To be a Supreme Being of Zahtaum nature is when one has achieved total Oneness of identity of EVER IS Non Existent substance. The nature of Zahtaum is Love, the highest quality and intensity of perfect Love that is attainable. That Love is a fusion of supreme qualities: of Wisdom, Gratitude, Compassion, Power... A Supreme Being of Zahtaum level of Completion is perfectly fused with the Totality. Such a Being we name an **HIMMZAANON**: one who has fulfilled Life's destiny. This is Perfection. When such Completion is attained, one is then both Beginning and End.

That Primary Zeroness, the ITNESS of First Beginning, is therefore maturing Itself. It is forever "living", moving, inexhaustible in its perpetual creativity, undergoing great cycles of transformation and transmutation of its Being in a never ending Process of giving forth, maturation and self renewal. That ITNESS of Primordial Zeroness produces Beings of a dimensional Reality whose ITNESS is of Eternal nature of Supreme Zeroness – the ultimate and final purpose: ZAHTAUM/HIMMZAANON.

THE BRIMONDA

We know that the Cosmos is vast, even from the view we have of it through our ordinary physical senses. Aided in these modern times by sophisticated mechanisms which human intelligence has devised to assist our further discovery, we increasingly receive ever greater knowledge of our world. We are regailed with more and more facts – astonishing facts concerning many aspects of life, including the sheer magnitude and scale of this whole manifest realm of existence.

Light, we are told, travels at approximately 186,000 miles per second. Astronomers further inform us that our Sun is a mere 93 million miles from Earth, taking but 8 minutes for its light to reach us; whereas Light from the nearest star to our Sun, Proxima Centauri, takes some 4.3 years to reach Earth. However it takes 60,000 years (I have also seen the estimation given as 100,000 years) for light to travel – at the rate of 186,000 miles per second – from but one side to the other of our own Galaxy, the Milky Way. And our galaxy is only one of some hundred thousand million galaxies which can be seen from Earth with the aid of modern telescopes; each of these hundred thousand million or so galaxies themselves containing some hundred thousand million stars apiece.

We are further told that our nearest galaxy neighbour is a mere 2 million light years distant from us in the vastness of space; whereas the Virgo cluster of galaxies (which we can see in our night sky) is some 50-60 million light years from Earth. Another cluster of galaxies, which Astronomers call the "Coma" cluster, are calculated to be some 250 million light years from us. However quasers (stellar objects with powerful sources of radio waves and other forms of energy) have been located which are reckoned to be up to 10 *billion* light years distant from Earth...

Yet all this only speaks of what is local to us, of what is on our own doorstep so to speak. Even so, the ordinary human mind can scarcely comprehend, can only vaguely conceptualise such vastness. How phenomenal therefore (and, initially, mind shattering) has been my own viewing of the Brimonda seen with the "eye" of supra physical vision: seen with the vision of a deeper internal dimensional nature and therefore being of an internal order of experience freed from the ordinary sensory restrictions of this physical level of existence.

With such internal vision I have seen that in fact thousands of millions of galaxies such as our own comprise but one **Universe**; and there are billions of other such Universes as our own in Existence, each of which is composed of thousands of millions of galaxies.

I have observed the great body of galaxies comprising our own Universe to have a fish like constellatory form – a form shaped more like that of the larger sea mammals such as the Whale – but with four finlike appendages, two each side of the body... two short ones on its underside and two longer ones towards its rear. This great body of our Universe comprised as it is of innumerable galaxies (each galaxy being comprised of countless stars), is propelled by its fins and moves in space; such movement in space involving cosmic Time of such vast duration as to be incomprehensible to our human understanding. Positioned some three quarters of the way along one of the longer fins at the rear of this our Universe is the vast conglomeration of galaxies visible from our Earth. But to give some idea of its enormity, visualise the millions of galaxies seen from this Earth as occupying merely the space which would be taken up by something the size of a tennis ball positioned on one of the fins in relation to a creature, which in illustrative model form, is some six feet in length and two feet in depth.

The centre of the body of this colossal Universe is composed of smaller, less brilliant, galaxies of stars than those forming its outer crust. The outer encrustation of stars is brilliant; but it is the head of this great cosmic creature which is radiant with the most brilliant of galactic conglomerations.

I have further perceived that millions of such Universes make up but one building block or section of another, incomparably more vast cosmic creature which in TAYOZAAN is named a **Mahaverse**. The Mahaverse is composed of millions of such building blocks or sections, each building block or section being composed of millions of Universes. This cosmic creature has form which, for want of better description, I have likened to the shape of a seal cub. The Mahaverse so viewed from the vantage point of internal vision, was seen to be that which contains our own Universe. It is seen to be very young. In human terms it appears to be but weeks old, only at the commencement of its life. With the seeing was the knowledge that our Mahaverse is still growing; and this great cosmic form moves within the space of its own host, just as the Universes move in space within the body of the Mahaverse. Our Mahaverse's host is a yet more vast cosmic Being which I have named an **Ohomverse**.

In fact many millions of Mahaverses are contained within each of those even more collosal cosmic Beings, the Ohomverses. The Ohomverse is seen to be crescent shaped.

There are many millions of Ohomverses within the **Brimonda**. The Brimonda is the Total Body of Existence and is global in form, composed of the crescent shaped Ohomverses. But it is seen that this total Body of manifest Life is yet itself also a very young Being not yet matured, requiring Completion. The whole Brimonda is still growing. It is expanding with new creations and its whole content is also maturing.

We are of the Brimonda and the Brimonda is of us. Our physical bodies are of the matter of the Brimonda. We are composed of the substance, forces and energies of the Brimonda. There is interaction and mutual dependancy at all levels of Life within its great Body. The Brimonda, the whole manifest world of Existence, is part of our Selfhood. We can come to know this for ourselves as our own experience: this Oneness with our Brimonda.

* * * *

With the Light of the stars, with the Light of the Universes, is a Blackness. The Blackness is equal in quantity to the Light. Although black, the Blackness itself shines.

At the time this was viewed, I saw just the shining dark Cosmos, the black counterpart of this manifest world of Matter. With the seeing was the knowledge that this is the balancing counterpart of physical matter, positioned in its own finite space. The stars, the Universes, were not themselves visible to my internal vision when the Blackness was seen; but I just knew that they were also there. The Black counterpart of the Cosmos also moves; but it moves at a vastly slower rate – "slowness" of course being relative to the enormous scale of Cosmic Time.

The whole Brimonda possesses this Black Counterpart.

*   *   *   *

Such vision of the vast Body of the Brimonda was experienced not all at once but section by section over a period of some two years. If I had not seen it section by section, my mind, my human nervous system, could not have absorbed or accepted the enormity of it all. As it was, each stage of the seeing was by no means easy to accept. First of all I saw the vast cosmic body of our own Universe. Later, seeing that there are in fact millions of such Universes in but one gigantic Maḥaverse (of which there are in turn millions) had the effect of reducing me for a time to a state of near traumatised despair. I did not wish to see or know any more. It was enough. Being such a tiny particle of life within such an incomprehensible vastness, one felt annihilated.

Each vision was shared with my wife as it occurred – but magnificent and awesome though the experiences were, we both initially felt the same sense of our relative total insignificance in the face of such magnitude. So overwhelming was the realisation of the enormity of Creation that for a time we both lost heart. We questioned the point of it all; but eventually the totality of the vision was able to be comprehended, gradually absorbed and finally accepted by our minds and hearts – not merely just accepted but responded to with neither timidity, fear nor rejection. The vision came, on the contrary, to be accepted with a deep response not just of appreciation but of loving gratitude. It opened and expanded with fresh intelligence our comprehension of Reality. It matured the Light within us with a wonderfully enhanced sense of and capacity for magnanimity of Being.

We bless the Brimonda. Our destinies are inextricably intertwined. We see the need for incarnation, for us to be subjected to the experience of living in this magnificent (albeit often fearsomely harsh) manifest World of Existence, for it is our necessary field of experience, providing the means by which our individual destinies as well as that of the Totality of Life can be fulfilled.

The vastness of external Existence is no greater than the vastness of the internal Eternal dimensional Reality; and our possibilities equal the vastness of both.

ANTI LIFE FORCES

Light, Darkness and Matter form a welded state of Existence. With the "Light": the animating Force of Life – is its dark nature of Opposition. Anti Life Force was within the commencement of Matter for it was within the first creative thrust. It is a necessary constraining, opposing and destructive Force within Life's nature, within the quality of the Force which is Life. Manifest Existence could not have been, could not have commenced and maintained its long process of evolution without the "Anti" Force of Life. Without it there would be unrestrained expansion and that expansion would be stagnant, a growth without spine, without substance of maturity. Without opposition, conscious intelligence would not increase. Our own Light – which is our Self, an individualised spark of Life – cannot have come to be what it is, cannot have matured its Being, without its dark opposition.

Light was the originator of Darkness and Darkness was the originator of Light in the Eternal ITNESS state of the First Beginning of all Beginnings. And all subsequent new creations which have occurred and are continuing to occur from Completed Beings within the maturing process of the vast Brimonda have had and will continue to have its new darkness of Anti Life Force within it.

Creation is a purposeful act. To produce "pure" Light is not the way creation can expand or mature purposefully. The Blessing from the Completed Being of an Himmonda which produces new creation is magnificent, wonderful and highly purposeful. Such a Blessing is from an immense quality and surge of Loving Gratitude but darkness is part of the strong driving force within that cosmically procreative act.

Anti Life Force can be said to be as a germ within the very Beginning. Therefore all ensuing Life is impregnated with it. As it is part of the very structure of manifest Existence from the beginning and has *purpose* in that it provides the friction of opposition necessary for Life's development, we must see that it needs to be acknowledged, fully faced, understood and its purpose realised.

The Anti Life Force has in fact become diversified into a vast plurality of Forces. These become entities or "personalities" which can enter and inhabit human beings and other sentient creatures. Some are our own creations, in which case they belong to and exist within the individual in whom they have been formed. Whether they belong to us or originate outside of us they exert strong influence, affecting our states of being and behaviour. These dark forces and their influences have to be constructively utilised – and conquered. To leave the Anti Life Forces to flourish is a recipe for self destruction. If they are not controlled our destiny becomes one of agony instead of one of fulfilment. If allowed to become powerful beyond the limits of its purpose, the Anti Life Force assumes dominant control and becomes an evil to Life.

The Force of Anti Life has a right to grow. In fact as Life expresses itself in manifestation and expands, so does the Anti Life Force or opposing aspect of Life's nature become stronger, more diversified and intelligent. The Law of Life operates for Darkness as it does for Light, but if the intelligent Light permits imbalance and allows Darkness to proliferate and dominate, instead of the grandness and perfection which should be, there will be disaster and degradation: an abysmal existence of sheer pain. As we know, such conditions of abysmal darkness do occur, are occurring and have always occurred to greater or lesser degree from time to time and from place to place on this Earth.

There are positive ways of dealing with Life's dark forces. They must not be reacted to negatively. To despise or hate them only stimulates overgrowth of the very Anti Life forces we wish (and need) to conquer. It is indeed real education of rare value which gives understanding of these matters and teaches how to control and develop Life to its purposeful Completion.

* * * *

The forever opposing Anti Life Force, both within the individual human being and within the whole Anti Life Force field of Existence, is of us and constitutes a level of our Selfhood. It is our grossest Eighth level of Selfhood. Everyone, no matter who they may be, must be aware of its influence. Even at times when perhaps just sitting quietly at home, even when endeavouring to ennoble oneself in meditation or when at prayer, wrong thoughts will arise in the mind provoking negative feelings. Such thoughts and feelings may be relatively innocuous – perhaps of only a mildly uncharitable, resentful or rejecting nature, or merely shallowly inappropriate – but are nevertheless unseemly and disturbing. Some thoughts and feelings which project themselves into our awareness may in some people be definitely bad, quite vile, even evil. Such unbidden intrusions occur and reoccur. We may be shocked and dismayed and try to clamp down our thoughts but find ourselves powerless to stop them. Many of us become so used to these promptings of the Anti Life Forces (which are made upon our already existing weaknesses) that they are agreed with, accepted as one's legitimate thoughts and feelings and are fuelled to further expression with perhaps satisfaction or actual enjoyment. If that occurs we then act from this base level and can be stimulated to many kinds of negative behaviour. The Anti Life Forces then become progressively ever more deeply attached to our Being and impregnate the components (or characteristics) carried within the Light of our *Life*. The Anti Life Forces – together with our higher, noble qualities – thus become part of our essential Self, continuing with us from incarnation to incarnation until they may eventually come to be dealt with and our Being is freed.

Humanity tries to explain away its negativity as being due to this or that cause but we cannot blame genetic inheritance for all our imperfections (nor, of course, conversely should our genes be given credit for all our attributes); neither in all honesty can we blame poor circumstances of life as an excuse for bad behaviour. Our level of Being determines our actions.

* * * *

Three types of characteristic typify the Anti Life Force. One can recognise these characteristics in the human being in what can be categorised as our Weak Self, our Opposing Self and our Demonic Self.

1. The weak Self has no moral stamina but takes the least line of resistance. It will say "No" when it should say "Yes". It will say "Yes" when it should say "No". The weak Self lacks courage. Fear is its strong emotion. It cringes from and pushes away what it does not feel able to face up to. It will not be able to stand up for itself nor be of help to others in their time of need. It is mean and of narrow vision. Slothfulness and ignorance are also its hallmark. It is apathetic. It procrastinates. It vacillates. It follows without mind of its own. The weak Self seeks escape – but it cannot, of course, escape the

pain of itself unless and until it be transformed. It will succumb to the lure of alcohol or drugs or try to lose itself in sexual gratification, and it will lack sense of responsibility in succumbing to these gratifications. It will usually find and blame some cause outside of itself for such weakness. It is self-pitying, unable to overcome, lacking energy in the grip of laziness. The weak Self is full of confusion, fatalistic and prone to superstition. It lacks joy or healthful ambition. The weak Self is that in us which lacks confidence, which holds one back with sense of inadequacy, ineptitude and inability to cope. From the weakness of its own sense of inadequacy and lack of self-worth, it will be envious and jealous of others. Paradoxically the weak Self in operation is a very strong force.

2. The opposing Self is the opposition which pressures us in our daily lives. It is encountered both within ourselves and within the external world with which we interact. It engenders frustration and anger, fuelling aggressive behaviour. It anchors, blocks and retards our internal and external progress, producing obstacles in our path so that we frequently feel undermined and thwarted in our efforts towards achievement. Even in more mundane ways most of us will recognise the irritating kinds of opposition which are common to us all: the extra financial pressures upon us when we are least in a position to bear them or just when we are trying to save some money; the missing item which has been hidden from view (seemingly by some gremlin-like activity) just when one cannot spare the time to search for it; the parking space which gets taken by someone else just when one is about to manoeuvre towards it; the hindrances in your path which cause you to lose that train or bus; the van that stops just at a point to block your vision when you need to see to cross the road... The list can be endless. We all experience the disruptive

effects of the wrong word spoken or the wrong action taken – or the word spoken or action which is taken at the wrong time. Many of us live through times of strong opposition when one thing after another goes so badly wrong we feel as though Life has a personal vendetta against us, leaving us perhaps damaged or bereaved, hurt, perplexed, harassed and stressed. The opposing Self is also ignorant but more energetically so than the weak Self. It is rejecting, does not wish to align with another's point of view and therefore repetitively causes disharmony in relationship. Like the weak aspect of our Self it is unreliable. It digs its heels in stubbornly, is dominating and strives for supremacy over others. The power of opposition in life is very strong, a force which it must be quite obvious to us all constantly besets us to greater or lesser degrees. We take it for granted, in fact, that our lives are obstructed by difficulties.

3. The demonic Self shows itself in acts of extreme negative egoism. Even if not expressed in outward behaviour, it can be recognised in thoughts and emotions of hatred, cruelty, masochism, sadism or perversion. The demonic forces attach themselves to, stimulate and make use of the sexual energies and urges, inciting to rape and indecencies of behaviour. It enslaves with strong, unquenchable sexual appetite. The demonic Self fantasises unhealthfully, is profane, will express itself in ugly or bizarre ways in its choice of environment, clothing, hairstyle or ornamentation. It likes to tattoo and pierce the flesh with objects, with studs, metal rods and rings through the nose, lips, eyebrows and other parts of the anatomy, not seeing this as a despoiling of the body but as a satisfying expression which inflates the ego. The demonic Self sees itself with different eyes to those seeing with the qualities of Light. The demonic Self expresses itself through raucous unmelodic music and voice. It hungers for gross excitation of the senses.

It stimulates the body's movements with its base quality of energy, revealing itself in the way a person walks, dances or generally disports himself. The demonic nature seeks self aggrandisement, is cocky and rebellious, despises others, is cynical, is full of destructive criticism. It denegrates, having no feeling or wish to uplift, to support and encourage or be sympathetic. It lies. It has no conscience. It has neither remorse nor regret. It is without pity or sensitivity so that it will hurt another without qualm. It is responsible for all kinds of abuses, taking advantage of the weak, the young, the vulnerable. It is capable of torture and murder. It exploits life. In its aggressiveness and ruthlessness it is puffed up with false pride and is arrogant. It results in feelings and the expression of nationalistic and racial superiority. It stimulates strong feelings of racist rejection. It manifests itself as brazenly loutish, disporting itself with uncaring ignorance, finding amusement in the base. It is greed and selfishness personified.

* * * *

The total Anti Life Self within each individual human being, composed of a mixture of weakness, opposition and the demonic – to immensely varying extents within each and every one of us – has cunning intelligence and seeks to be the dominant force within us. It seeks to take total control. The more the individual actually agrees with and follows its urges, the more we submit by default through sheer weakness to the stimulation of the Anti Life forces – whether it be we are energised directly by our own negativities or whether we succumb to negative provocation from the outside world – the more powerful it becomes. For the more habitual is our agreement with or submission to the urges of the Anti Life Force the more indelible is the imprint of its nature upon the individual and the more difficult then is the task of overcoming, of mastering its destructive activity.

The objective of the Anti Life Force is to take full possession of the individual; and it is seen to do so, in some instances perhaps succeeding only momentarily, in other cases succeeding in remaining in long term possession and control. In some instances it destroys the person so possessed. It can drive one to one's death.

The Anti Life Forces cause us restlessness of mind, disquiet in our feelings, inability to concentrate or to rest peacefully. They can be the cause of insomnia and certain kinds of illness including many mental problems. No creature is free from the influence of Life's dark forces. No Church, Mosque, Temple or other place of worship is without them; in fact they abound in such places. No aesthetic, no human however refined, noble or sincerely motivated is immune from them. If we are honest, even though it be to our chagrin, none of us can be best pleased at all times with our inner content. And, as has already been observed, at its more destructive depths of expression the Anti Life Force produces in some of us thoughts, feelings and actions which are truly monstrous. There are many who have no qualm, no feeling of guilt or compassion in harming or butchering other sentient life forms, although it must be obvious to them that these creatures experience fear and pain. Some actually find pleasure and an upsurge of strength from such pursuit. This is also apparent behind the veneer of respectability of those who pursue bloodsports. The truly demonic enjoy witnessing fear and pain and will set out to cause it. Even less is there concern or care for trees and the living body of the planet overall which is seen merely to exist for exploitation and self gratification.

Anti Life Force causes excessive appetite whether it be for wealth and possessions, food, fame or pleasure. Unnatural sexual practices to gratify the senses are inspired by the Anti Life forces. There is satisfaction in degradation.

Even the kind of food sought out and relished is that which energises the negative aspects of one's nature. The eating of meat, for instance, fuels the excitable negative qualities; and with the eating is also incurred not only the physical but the karmic results of the fear and pain endured by the slaughtered animal.

Supposedly "civilised" human beings who are well educated, in the ordinary academic sense, sanction or themselves physically carry out vivisection and other hideous experiments on vulnerable animals who have no choice in the matter... creatures who, at the mercy of the greater strength and cleverness of we "more evolved" beings, are forced to pay an horrendous price on our behalf for possible advantage to mankind. These creatures are evolving life forms like ourselves, at different levels of sensitivity and intelligence, for which we should feel strong sense of responsibility but humankind permits them to be experimented on, imprisoned and piteously helpless in laboratories all over the world. Year after year millions of animals are caused to experience a living hell of fear and suffering in the name of "human progress". The medical and scientific worlds justify this as being morally vindicated, an acceptable sacrifice (enforced though it be) of less evolved life forms for the eventual possible and hoped for benefit of the human race, even if much of the time all that is yielded is the repetitious practice of techniques and a little more practical knowledge for the individuals concerned in the experimentation. So long as some aesthetic or good motivation for such experimentation can be advanced, it seems to be taken as read that the end must justify the means. Hard logic, the well developed intellect of level only of this material world, which lacks depth of quality of the Light within, is indeed dangerous. Sensitivity is easily dulled or even completely closed off by a consuming pursuit for knowledge. Just the average, unintellectual human being will be more alive to such an imbalance in values and feel instinctive horror at activity such as animal experimentation. How can we in all conscience justify receiving benefit at cost of the pain and mutilation of other creatures?

The developing intellect standing alone, lacking wisdom, without qualities of love, gratitude and compassion leaves us dehumanised; and it is very often such imbalanced people who are in positions of power.

The Anti Life Forces enter the various fields of increasing human development and progress in equally increasing clever and sophisticated ways. The "great" leaders, the conquesting warriors of history, were fired by strong "ideals" which were pursued relentlessly – and that very persistence has been admired as strength of character for in truth such force of energy does cause things to happen – but how much sheer destruction, bloodshed and misery has littered the paths of their passage. Adolf Hitler was fired by an "ideal" which was doomed to activate immense darkness, for his Light was so little developed in internal quality of Being. Force attracts like force and Hitler, in common with other such zealots, found affinity with many of similar ambition and calibre of being as himself. A mass of people can easily be caught up in a force field of emotion. Such energy surges through a mass like electric power. It is tangible. It can be felt to ebb and flow and rise to crescendos of power within a crowd. This fact will be recognised by anyone who has enthused with the mass at a concert or sporting event or who has experienced a demonstration or riot. In the case of Nazi Germany, Hitler seemingly quite easily managed to convince many that his ideal of an elite master race justified any means whether the means involved the elimination of anything or anybody seen to stand in the way of actualising his vision. Many were quite prepared to treat other human beings as mere garbage to be disposed of without pity or mercy, to clear the path towards his imagined utopia. This was indeed an example of the Anti Life Force at work, infiltrating and deluding the human mind to rationalise and justify the most diabolical and horrifying of behaviour.

We can surely see from past experience that whenever we act from cold reason without balancing qualities of love, wisdom and compassion, we produce misery.

The old adage that the way to hell is paved with good intentions is indeed true. The cunning of the Anti Life Force does make use of some goodness to beguile the human heart and mind to accept its promptings as correct, but it is insidious in its cleverness and lures the unwary into avenues which bear no resemblance to goodness. One therefore needs to be acutely vigilant and cautious at all times.

* * * *

The driving motivation of the Anti Life Self within us is to take over our Mind and nervous system so that it may live and expand its power; and it will fight with all its cunning to keep us in ignorance of its presence *and of our ability to overcome it*, for it knows that internal development of our Light will be its death. It is a Jekyll and Hyde situation, a battle between the opposing polarities within the world: a battle between our Light and the Anti Life Forces which function within our own bodies, within the world and within our Zero dimensional depths – a battle more profound and important than most realise for it is truly a question of survival. Either the Anti Life Forces win or we do.

The conflicting aspects of our Selfhood belong to us and are functioning according to their respective natures. If we intelligently co-operate with Life's purpose and try to deal with our Anti Life Self content, some battles may well be lost along the way for the fight is far from easy; but with sincere persistence, the war itself can eventually be won. The resultant peace, strength and freedom in the victory will more than justify the struggle.

Life's opposition is both a means and a spur to internal achievement but it must ultimately be totally conquered, otherwise we will find ourselves the vanquished. In the internal dimensions, as in the physical jungle of plant and animal life, there is a relentless urge and seeking for opportunity in the pursuit of survival and maximum fulfilment. At the end of the day our Light within must therefore rise to a position of supremacy and power, when it can properly utilise and master the Forces of Life to highest purpose.

* * * *

The Anti Life Forces can – for a time at least – present themselves to us in beauteous form. They can project themselves to us as angels, stimulating feeling of loving emotion, producing delightful colours, sounds and odours to beguile with pretence of goodness. An Anti Life Force can also appear to us in its real form, which is ugly and deformed, its vibration producing instinctive fear. It is of murky colour with harsh voice and is malodorous.

Spiritualists and Mediums therefore need to be very careful. They may be unaware to what they open themselves and with what they can interact. The Anti Life Forces can enter their receptivity pretending to be the spirits of those who have died. They can present the appearance of anyone they choose and may well convey some correct information or even some acceptable guidance to convince of their credibility; but what is conveyed is mostly superficial and of no help to us, the only benefit being to give some the comfort of assurance that there is a Zero world beyond the material life we know. But even that "benefit" is fraught with danger as it encourages the naive to continue to open themselves towards the influence of the Anti Life Forces in pursuit of further experience.

No protection is afforded by such things as joss sticks or incense. The Anti Life forms are seen to merely play with the smoke from the burning incense, merging in and out of it as it rises into the air. Some may believe they have a special friend in such an entity but one should be extremely cautious of opening oneself to or encouraging any such visitation.

Many believe in UFO's – the so called Unidentified Flying Objects – to be visitations from highly advanced finite beings from outer space, but if they were beings from the manifest world of matter they would need to have machinery capable of moving at speeds far faster than the speed of light to cover the vast distances involved in interplanetary or inter galactic travel. I have experienced such visitations so do not dismiss as imagination the experiences reported by others. However, I soon realised that what was observed was not of a finite nature but was manifestation from the

Zero dimensions; and that the beings projected into my awareness were of Anti Life Force nature. They may masquerade as friends of ours but they are not. They are able to appear and to disappear again just as rapidly into their own dimensional sphere. Their "vehicles" are their Anti Life Force structures. They can interfere with and have affect upon both material substance and living creatures. Those I have seen have had spindly deformity of form. They project bodies of dull off-white, yellowish, pale green unpleasant hues. I have seen these beings disporting themselves surrounded by a haphazardly moving formation of what gave the appearance of being vari-coloured fairy light bulbs. Sometimes they became invisible within the formation of lights but I knew that they were still there. Some have animal like shape, but mostly they try to impersonate human form to be acceptable to our human vision. Some have mere indications for nose or mouth. Some have eyes like outsized goggles.

The eyes convey more of their evil nature even than their bodies – but the clever Anti Life Force entities can, as mentioned above, disguise themselves (temporarily at least) to assume acceptable or even beautiful human form. The more "advanced" Anti Life Force entities can even present beauty through their eyes – if only for a limited time – although for most the eyes, if revealed, are an instant giveaway as to their true nature. However their "home" within the Zero dimensions (whether it be within the human being or elsewhere) is a place which is murky and dirty, full of vomit-like mire; a place which is repellent to the Self of any Being with the qualities of Light but which is natural to an entity of Anti Life Force nature.

The way to actually annihilate the Anti Life Self and the structure in which it lives, has to be taught.

The first line of defence against the influence of the Anti Life forces lies in understanding. Intelligence has power. The practical methods of TAYOZAAN use that intelligent power. Intelligent discrimination with understanding is essential, for the Anti Life aspect of reality is constantly defending and consolidating and endeavouring to expand its hold. It is an arch disseminator of the truth, a master of deflection with half truths; a deceiver to which one can easily fall prey. Hence we make mistakes and, inevitably, we develop faults. This is the human condition. But our faults and weaknesses are our Achilles heels, prime targets for stimulation by the Anti life forces; so we must beware, be on our guard, constantly evaluating ourselves and monitoring our responses to life with all the sincerity we can muster.

* * * *

It is truly vital that we face the reality of the Anti Life Forces which assuredly have very real affect upon the lives of each and every one of us. It is only too easy to succumb to its perhaps less obvious and insidious influence. We find ourselves locked in attitudes of mind, imprisoned by emotional moods from which we cannot readily escape. So we become progressively more negative in the misery of not being able to deal with our condition, even if we try; or we obstinately cement our attitudes and moods, maintaining they are justified.

Our relationships with others are particularly fruitful hunting grounds for the opposing forces. We are either triggered by our own Anti Life nature to speak or act in a certain negative way or our Anti Life content is stimulated to action by vibrations from another's Anti Life content. We readily react – negatively – to anger or irritation directed towards us and to any real or imagined rejection. Similar negative attitudes and emotions which lurk within us rise up to join the fray and before we know it antlers are locked, metaphorically speaking, like stags at bay. As at times of combat, the body responds with hormonal releases in readiness for fight or flight, there is temporarily a surge of energy and often these strong vibrations give feeling of power and satisfaction to the ego in the moment; but that surge of energy creates strong thought and feeling which is registered within, fixing a behavioural pattern within the memory and so paving the way for replay of similar response next time a like situation arises. Each time the same buttons are pressed we find ourselves mechanically repeating the same sad negative reactions.

As our psyche needs stimulation to feel more fully alive, we tend to accept or even seek out the negative if we find negativity feeds that hunger. Strangely, such emotions as anguish and fear are perversely "enjoyed" by some. Even ill-health (real or imagined) can be satisfying and a person may be loth to relinquish the condition, it being a reliable subject for self-interest and a plausible way of attracting the attention and concern of others.

Whilst it may not be admitted (and may well be strenuously denied) unhappy conditions and emotions are often "life" to the ego. This kind of sickly perverse enjoyment is seen in the sado-masochist. It is seen in the paedophile and in those who seek out sensual titillation in other sordid pursuits and low-life environments. Little do such people suspect, by agreeing to such urges, what danger they are in and what a terribly hard job they will have to face in due course to free themselves from the unrelenting grasp of the dark forces which have ensnared them into such behaviour, which have come to possess their being and which will continue to pursue them both during life *and beyond the grave*. They see no farther than the present moment of their perverse enjoyment. But there is no escape. The chilling fact is that the time will come when they will have to know and face what it is they have allowed into their being. They will have to face just what it is they have nurtured within themselves in the enjoyment of their ignorance and depravity. No-one would consciously ever elect to be in their shoes. The cost to be borne, the pain to be suffered is fearsome. The burden is heavy.

The Anti Life Forces will continue to work on all our weaknesses, on our faults and on our guilts. Most of us prefer to place the blame for our own negative content on causes outside of us. We readily blame genetic inheritance or place the blame on some negative influence or happening experienced in our childhood, but the buck has to stop right here with oneself. We are ultimately the ones responsible for our own behaviour.

So, beware. Take heed of the company you keep. Do not intentionally place yourselves close to negative influences of the depraved, the ignorant, the aggressive, the foolish and selfish, the haughty and proud, the uncaring and the ungrateful. The task is uphill enough as it is without being dragged down by those of poor quality of being who have no intention of trying to be otherwise. But, of course, should they wish to change and are prepared to be helped, be compassionate and try to uplift. However be careful. You will need to be wise and strong in your dealings with them, otherwise you may find yourself damaged by their weakness and negativity.

* * * *

The adage of the three monkeys: "See no evil; Hear no evil; Speak no evil" is re-written in TAYOZAAN. We make the more constructive statement: "See, hear of, speak against and deal with evil". So much there is of it in this world.

The Zaans of TAYOZAAN are not pacifists. The philosophy of TAYOZAAN teaches action: constructive action. In relation to the Anti Life Forces it teaches that the internal fight to master evil needs, when warranted, to be translated into physical force. One must never weakly present the other cheek to manifestation of the force of evil, for its response will only be to crush one ever harder. In this life one normallv finds that the proferred "other cheek" gets slapped too. Internal strength from the quality of the Light within, combined with strong external action is necessary. It is of little effect to be strong in one direction only. Strength both internally and in outward expression is vital.

We have a long and continuing history of the horrors humanity is capable of inflicting on its own kind – quite beyond the behavioural capacity of any other life form on this planet. The fearful reality is that mankind, whilst walking the Earth in human form, can be filled with and manifest from *subhuman* force. That force can be one of sheer evil.

We tend not to want to acknowledge the reality of the existence of Life's dark forces. Most of us prefer to brush the evidence of its existence (which evidence stretches way back into the far distant past of history and patently continues with us to the present day) under the proverbial carpet, but if we do that nothing will ever really change but will continue as before, century after century. The position can even worsen. We must not, therefore, allow to be forgotten, nor must we condone, excuse or be apathetic towards the painfully stark facts of mankind's past and present inhumanities; nor must we ever abandon others to yet further similar terrible fate in the future. We must determine unrelentingly to fight the dark forces until our last breath - and beyond...for our Life continues beyond death.

We must never surrender. We must never give up. It is but our ordinary duty to Life.

THE HUMAN POSITION

Let us try to picture our human position as it relates to the external and internal realities of our lives.

We find ourselves existing within a physical body on a physical planet within the whole vast Cosmos of finite matter.

Our physical form houses a subtler body of an internal dimensional nature. It belongs to that which TAYOZAAN names the Stabilising Dimension. Many know this dimension as the "spirit" world. That subtler Stabilising or spirit form functions through the physical body. It is in effect the blueprint of the physical body. The Stabilising body can be seen with internal vision and it looks similar to the physical body but in some it appears older, in others more youthful than its physical form.

We can readily understand and accept that life forms such as trees and plants possess Life of an invisible, subtler nature than that of mere physical matter. Even more so can it be understood and accepted that the more animate and intelligent life forms of animals – including of course ourselves: humankind, the most highly evolved of the animal kingdom – are possessed of Life of an internal dimensional nature.

It is clear that the Stabilising Self is much more developed within animals than it is within plant life and that this internal life force or "personality" is more developed within the human being than it is within animals. But it is not so readily understood that *all* physical matter has its Zero dimensional content. Every physical form, be it the furthermost star in the cosmos, our sun, the moon, the body of this living Earth itself and every mountain, rock, river, ocean or any other construct of nature – even made objects such as houses, cars and other artefacts fashioned from physical matter – are possessed of a Stabilising dimensional content or nature. This can be observed as fact from the Stabilising point of view.

The Stabilising Being of the Sun can be contacted. The Sun's Being is capable of travelling away from its physical form within the Stabilising dimension and it can be observed and communicated with by one's own Stabilising content.

The Sun is a great Being who has shown itself to be a strong and loyal friend. This Being has visited me to convey support and friendship at times of personal need, coming in the roundness and colour of the evening setting sun.

Our Moon was found to be a timid shy Being who for some reason was in an entrapped position, bound and unable to move.

The Stabilising spirit forms of rivers and trees bear (respectively) a wispily watery or tree-like Stabilising form which can likewise move away from their physical vehicles to some extent before returning to fully inhabit their grosser, manifest forms.

* * * *

As we know, the physical body of man has a physical brain as its central animating organ. The central organ of the Stabilising or spirit content of the human being is Mind. Mind expresses itself through the brain-controlled physical body and is influenced and affected by its experience of and its interaction with this living, ever moving external manifest world. Our Mind also interacts with our Light. Mind is therefore additionally affected by and is affecting the depth of our Selfhood. It is a two-way flow in two directions: interaction towards and from the external world and interaction towards and from the internal dimensional reality of the Zero worlds.

It is Mind, by its intelligent interaction with both our Light and the external world which can cause its own maturity and that of our Light.

That Light, the Life "Seed" of our Existence which is the essence of what we *are*, is of the Unutterable creative dimensional nature and is the true "I" which should be the master within – but our Light is initially relatively undeveloped. As has been explained, when fully developed the Unutterable Light is of a completely *eternal* nature. But until it has developed sufficiently, our essential Self of Light needs to continue incarnating into the manifest world, life after life, until it is able to remain in the Zero dimensional worlds following death of the physical body

The Stabilising Self does not reincarnate but after death of the physical body it, eventually, also dies – from the Stabilising dimension.

Death of the physical body occurs when the Unutterable Light (or whatever more advanced Zero dimensional level our Light may have achieved) withdraws and no longer animates it. Following death of the physical body one's Light may stay connected to its Stabilising Self for a time within the Zero worlds prior to either rebirth or continuation within the deeper dimensional planes of Zeroness if the Light has achieved sufficient affinity with the substance of that deeper dimensional level.

* * * *

Therefore it is Mind – as distinct from mere physical brain – which is the important connecting bridge between the internal and the external worlds. And it being the truly central organ of our functioning, the development of our Mind is therefore the key to hastening real evolutionary progress. A closed, undeveloped Mind is like a closed door which bars possibility of our achieving the kind of emancipation which can free us from many more lifetimes of return to this gross physical dimension. The developed or developing Mind is as an open or opening door to ever heightening intelligent connection with both the outer world of manifest existence to which we belong and its Zero dimensional reality. All aspects of Life comprise our natural potential heritage.

It is therefore Mind which is the instrument capable of building and maturing our Unutterable Light. It is the instrument which, the more it is itself refined, sharpened and developed, can eventually *transmute* the Unutterable Light into a Light of the Non Existent dimensional nature – and even beyond, for it can eventually transmute even a Selfhood of Non Existent quality into yet subtler dimensional depths. Such development is dependant upon our incarnations on this Physical plane to experience the maturing rigours of Existence.

It is vital that we understand how important is our life here in manifest form, for this physical world is the fertile environment within which Life achieves its multi dimensional evolution. For in fact both the external and the internal: the physical and the Zero dimensions, are aspects of but one purposeful Reality. But although the physical and supra physical are in truth one Reality, we have to make effort to enable that *Life* – which is the Light within each of us – to blossom into conscious unity of Being with all dimensions before we actually achieve that Reality, that matured Oneness of identity with the Allness. To move towards and eventually become possessed of such unity of Being our sense of I-ness needs to be centred within a supra physical Zero "substance" of Being; and such substance of Being has to be earned/developed.

* * * *

Many feel urge to seek their true "I-ness" or *identity* – something on which they can rely and which carries with it an inherent sense of self worth. But our individual identity can only be that which it actually *is* at any given point in time, for although the potential of the Timeless Zero worlds lies within our Seed of Existence, we are not yet of that quality until we have achieved it. Before it has been actually attained it remains merely our inherent potential.

Blind as we mostly are to our true possibilities, many seek from the superficial to find or acquire a heightened sense of identity. But by placing undue importance upon such "crusty" factors as one's race, nationality, culture, religion or other equally evanescent circumstance of birth, we can only reinforce our "personalities", so strengthening a superficial level of Selfhood, not achieving for ourselves a sense of truly valid identity. By emphasising such relatively unimportant outer circumstances of our lives we will not move in the direction which can produce nobility of true I-ness, nor therefore obtain for ourselves real satisfaction or sense of fulfilment which comes when a true "I" within us has been achieved with quality of appreciative expansiveness in magnanimity of compassion and wisdom. Sadly, to the contrary, the human condition hardly measures up to such description. We so often see (as history also confirms to have long been the case) that the false pride which accompanies emphasis on any particular race, nationality, culture or religion, causes division, fostering attitudes of superiority and, most damagingly, *rejection* of those of differing cultures and race.

So many of us on this Earth are still unawakened to the simple overriding truth of the matter that we are all merely human beings belonging to but one body of humanity sharing a similar range of human joys, difficulties and woes during the short span of time we have here. In common with everyone else, we happen to be currently inhabiting this tiny planet of ours, moving as it is in the vastness of space with us all aboard. The present incarnation of each of us happens to be coinciding here at this particular point in Time in a long ongoing process of Life. Yet, sadly and dangerously, some hardly recognise our common humanity at all, such is the imbalance of viewpoint; such is the blinkered vision.

When one's viewpoint is from one of the Zero dimensions it will be seen how irrational it is to place oneself above others, to be superiorly "proud" to be of any particular colour, race or nationality, cult or religion. A stance of superiority separates. It fosters an elitist attitude which denigrates others and leads to rejection. So much of the negativity we experience in this life results from rejection.

To consider oneself superior for being of male or female gender, for age to look down upon youth (or, conversely for youth to despise the aged) is both irrational and unjust. To place oneself on a pedestal because one occupies a particular position or station in life or enjoys a higher status of wealth or education than others, is not only ignoble but such a stance reveals our immaturity. The quality required is not *pride* but *gratitude*. Simply to be “grateful” towards life in compassionate acceptance of our common humanity would transform existence on Earth.

We do indeed need to have sense of our own worth but we are not “worthy” unless we value every other living being.

Our time here in each incarnation is short and our circumstances of life are only temporary. Life is in a complex state of flux, in constant movement, and is therefore fraught with uncertainty. We are all at differing stages of evolution. And how we perform in this life matters, for this one life is not the end of the line. We take our content with us into the future. There is no escape from oneself.

Soon life will move us on and we may well find ourselves suffering and enjoying quite different circumstances in our next incarnation: perhaps having to experience a body of the opposite gender to that which we at present inhabit. We may well come to be born in another country, of another race, influenced by another culture, speaking a different language. We may then have to experience similar conditions to those whom in this present life we have reviled and despised. We may come to find ourselves in similar circumstances to those whom we at present envy – and may find ourselves having to bear the burden of similar responsibilities. We may come to find ourselves sharing another incarnation but in different relationship with those we have known – be they present loved ones, those with whom we have shared former lives, or be they past or present “enemies”.

Viewed thus, we can see that we are but the means, the avenue for further incarnation of other beings. We do not "own" our children. They are individuals in their own right with their own long past and their own future destinies who are only temporarily in our care. Parenthood and the nurturing and care of the young is a great responsibility – and a great opportunity for growth. It is therefore also a great privilege.

In some future incarnation we could achieve birth through one of the children who have been born to us in this present life; or we may already have been a child of theirs in a past incarnation. Equally our present children or grandchildren could have been – or may in future lives become – our grandparents, brothers, sisters, or perhaps spouses. The range of possibility is enormously wide.

Our past is stored within our essence, within the Seed of Existence within us – as also is all future possibility, *for we are Life, and Life is all possibility.*

* * * *

Our Light, our Seed of Existence is, therefore, multi Life. This being so, let us expand our thinking yet further to accept that we may well also have experienced past incarnations elsewhere than on this Earth – perhaps on planets in yet other Universes within this vast Brimonda. And our future destiny may be such that we could find ourselves reincarnated elsewhere than on planet Earth in a time yet to come. This is not mere surmise or imagination. Images have emerged, recalled from my Light's "memory" or essence, of terrains, buildings and animals of a quite different type to that which we experience here. These have been fleeting images but one knows they are memories of other worlds one has known.

You and I have already existed for countless millions of years, having evolved through countless births and deaths in a vast variety of forms – from that of the most simple celled and primitive at the commencement of our journey in the early stages of our Mahaverse's physical manifestion, to the complexity of form and degree of intelligence which we now possess. And we know not what we may yet come to experience, either whilst still in this existence or in some future incarnation.

* * * *

As already indicated, for me – as for many other people – reincarnation is no mere mental concept but a fact of life. It is not unique to human experience to recover from one's essence "memory" of previous existences. Such memories may only come forward into conscious awareness as fleeting images; just glimpses of one's past. For most it will no doubt be an unusual experience, not repeatable at will. That, at least, is true for me.

At various times I have had insights into my evolutionary progress, from which it is clear that Life never ***in****volves*. Life may take a long while to move forward but the evolutionary process does not permit a retrograding backward flow. Therefore once we have entered the human form we will not return as an insect or as an animal in a future incarnation (as is the belief of many) no matter how "inhuman" may have been our conduct and level of being during any particular human incarnation.

I have had swift glimpses of myself having lived a succession of lives in animal form. Some were unusual types of creature such as are not seen on this Earth. Of the kind of animals known to us on this planet, I was aware of having been either a lion or a tiger (the impression was not that clear) which was stalking a gazelle or some other small deerlike animal. And in another viewing the position was reversed and I saw myself to be a small deerlike creature quietly grazing. I looked up. Then came sudden blankness as I myself became the prey of a lion or tiger.

On a subsequent viewing I saw myself to have evolved into a primitive early humanoid type of creature. I recognised myself as one of a group. I was standing on the outer fringe of this group. We were moving our heads from side to side as if somewhat nervous or agitated, then with one accord we moved forward across the landscape, our muscular bodies walking strongly but primitively, the arms and shoulders being well in evidence as the shoulders also moved forward with the long stride of the legs.

On another viewing of myself as an early humanoid, this time I saw myself leading a group of similar creatures. We were all heading somewhere with seemingly singleminded, purposeful intent.

In all these viewings, one recognises oneself from the Light within the centre of the forehead and/or from the "atmosphere" of the creature. There is connection with that Light or atmosphere which one knows to be oneself.

In addition to having seen myself as a variety of animals and having glimpsed my entry into human form at primitive levels of humanity in times long past, I have also seen my first arrival onto this Earth. I saw that I had come from another Universe, having achieved status there in female form as a Queen or someone of royal power and dignity. This Queenlike figure of pleasant personality possessed African type physical features; and my entry into this Universe commenced with a series of births on this planet which occurred within the continent of Africa ... but this series of African incarnations were steeped in poverty. Here there was no status, no wealth or position of power. I saw that there were many births when I was left, mouth agape with unappeased hunger until a blank blackness engulfed me, signifying death. On occasions I was too weak even to feel hunger, so swiftly did death follow birth. Many times there was no impression of there being a Mother at hand to succour, to protect... no parents to grieve for me. In other incarnations I did survive. In one such life I glimpsed myself as an African male. I saw that I was poor, trying desperately to take care of my family. One child was very ill. I comprehended that I was one who worked hard to help and to please but that I was used by others and that my good nature was abused. Because I answered the demands of others I was not at home when my child died. I returned to find my son (or it may have been a daughter) dead. The stark reality of my position was seen too late and I was filled with remorse. The hurt was intense.

In another, later incarnation, I saw myself as an Englishman, of shortish stature but muscularly strong, clothed in a strangely coloured dark cloth which gave impression of poverty. I was standing upright in a small, cellarlike room, with my back touching the wall, arms down to my sides in abject stillness, an occasional tear silently wetting my cheeks. Although physically strong, here was a man feeling intense sadness and grief. But the emotions were well held within. I was moved by this impression of myself and curious to know what could have been the cause of such deep unhappiness; but I remain unknowing to this day except that on reconnecting with that memory I have been able to further intuit and feel that this Englishman was also Jewish and that he was deeply loyal to both his race and his religion. He was both English and Jewish to the bone. And I understood that his deep sorrow and hurt was somehow connected with his loyal heart. However, in a strange way, the disciplined pride which seemingly kept that grief privately to myself in that life, has kept me now from being able to penetrate and better understand the content of that past experience.

We are incarnated within various races and cultures. The gender in which we experience various lives may also change. I have mostly seen myself in the male gender. The only other viewing of myself which has been in female form was of a time when I was reincarnated as a Japanese woman. I saw myself as the wife of a Japanese nobleman. I had the impression that I endured a position of subservience to this nobleman who always appeared to be sitting on a high chair on a platform or dais above everyone else. He was clothed in cloth and metal. I felt confined in that place – and very unhappy. Amongst others in the room was a man who stood as if he were a guard. He was a kindly person whom I loved; and I know that he loved me. Whilst tending my husband's needs my mind and heart were with this man but the knowledge was with the viewing that we would never be able to be together in that life and that I died still in the position of unhappy wife to this Japanese nobleman.

I have seen myself to have lived several lives as Indian Maharajahs. Each time I had a somewhat similar face. It is with no sense of pride that I speak of this for I have seen that I was devious and manipulative in this role; of high cunning. I engineered conflicts in confident assurance of victory as my strategies were cleverly calculated in advance. I saw how I walked. I moved with distasteful arrogance.

I do not know the sequence in time in which these further incarnations on this Earth have taken place following my African experiences but another viewing which is of significance to me (and which brings me closer to my present incarnation) was of a life lived somewhere in Russia. It appeared that I was in some position of command in the Russian Army and on first viewing I was in the home of the young woman whom I wished to marry. I have a clear image of the house. It was a humble, countryfied wooden structure. I stood in a room which only contained a simple table and bench, talking to this lady's brother who was obviously a caring person, concerned for his sister's future happiness. The young woman herself emerged into the room, walking past me with gentle movement into the small kitchen beyond. She was very slender. She wore a long, straight, loose fitting dark gown as of oldfashioned times. As she passed there was an exchange between us of mutual sensitive yearning one towards the other. With the next viewing was the knowledge that we were by then husband and wife. It was wintertime and very cold. I saw myself leaving our home. I know that I had to leave urgently, seemingly on military duty. There was an atmosphere of apprehension, of caution. I was alone, riding on horseback when I was suddenly ambushed and killed. The end was swift. I do not know whether there were any children of that marriage but I know that that young Russian woman is today my wife in this our current life. And the young man who was my wife's brother in that Russian incarnation is today also still closely connected to us both. Our human destinies are intertwined.

Many times images from my past lives have shown a face which, although I knew to be my own, did not enable me to identify the race to which I had belonged – as if I was not of any particular country or specific race of people. I had the impression that these lives were lived as a refugee or wandering, stateless person, meagre of body, the eyes always searching, looking for a better life or just seeking survival.

Interestingly, when recollecting incarnations experienced in specific races, it is clear that one's life was then completely imbued with the atmosphere and "flavour" of the culture into which one had been born. I saw myself to have been Russian through and through when in my Russian incarnation and Eastern through and through when in my Japanese incarnation, just as I had been English and Jewish to the bone when an English Jew. When in midst of a new incarnation we are locked within the experience of our present environment. Within the confines and limitations of our current condition it is hard to imagine having been anything else. Therefore knowledge of past lives lived in such a wide diversity of circumstances, is liberating. It not only expands one's outlook but gives one a curious sense of freedom; freedom from the burden of one's superficial, temporary "identity". Freedom too from the ignorance of bias.

Some are loth to look backwards, but just as to reflect on history can illuminate, so too can knowledge of our past lives increase our intelligence and wisdom.

Life is by no means easy nor clear to our understanding but I know it to be highly purposeful. Armed with the breadth of knowledge earned to date in this long evolutionary journey – with its rich tapestry of past experiencing and future possibilities – one feels a great sense of fulfilment. With such fulfilment comes immense gratitude. Gratitude is an enormously important attitude of Mind and of one's Light, opening the way to yet greater possibilities. We can only live one life at a time but one life lived with quality of loving gratitude is of far greater value than a thousand ungrateful lives.

* * * *

Further with regard to the question of identity, the fact of the matter is that as our Unutterable Light matures into its eternal depths, our content changes. And as we become ever more that which is of substance of the Zero dimensional nature, our sense of identity therefore also changes. Our whole concept of Life changes. Our values alter and deepen and so does our viewpoint on Life. We come to discriminate differently. That which has hitherto been considered of greatest significance and importance now becomes seen in perspective of a wider and more subtle range of understanding. It is not that "existence" becomes unimportant or valueless but that the importance of the grosser, of the relatively superficial and evanescent, becomes absorbed by and into that which is greater. And this change is an ongoing process. The internal evolutionary process continues without cessation; apparently without boundary, without (in the finite sense) "end", into ever more refined depths of Zeroness.

However, although the quality of our substance of identity changes at each level of our development and although our understanding, perception of Truth and therefore our viewpoints change, not every person has the benefit of inner vision to "see" his or her own development but they will be in no doubt that inner change has occurred. One feels and knows that one's substance of being has changed; and something of that change of being will be sensed by others. Other people may even be magnanimous enough to acknowledge the difference, for a more profound connection with the Light within others begins to be established. Real contact can be made. Light more readily touches Light. And when there is mutual recognition – Light towards Light – there is naturally aroused greater respect for one another's depth and value. This brings togetherness, an opening of the heart to love and trust and greater peace and satisfaction in relationships. When our Light touches that within another, a connection is made which transcends all outer differences.

* * * *

Mind is the mysterious organ of the supra physical Stabilising Dimension. It is the vehicle for our Will, our intelligence and our qualities of being. Mind is that instrument which effects interaction between dimensions, that which enables the Seed of one's Existence to blossom, to express its creativity. It is the seat of that special kind of intelligence which can achieve development.

Mind, whilst invisible to the physical eye (for it is of the Stabilising Dimension), is seen with internal vision to have shape similar to that of the knitted Jewish skull cap and in relation to our body the Mind is in fact similarly positioned: towards the back of the head on top of the physical brain. Initially, in its relatively undeveloped state, the Mind looks like an untidy birds nest, a loosely woven grouping of "stalks" to which are attached (or from which protrude) something akin to bulbous ricelike grains. These bulbous ricelike grains vibrate, making a constant buzzing sound – like a myriad insects – night and day, without cessation. They all vibrate at differing tonal levels of sound. The colour of the relatively undeveloped Mind is grey to off-white. As the Mind achieves development, becoming ever more disciplined and refined, the loosely woven "bird nest" like grouping becomes increasingly more firmly knit, orderly and neat and its base also becomes smoothly compacted. Its base progressively darkens and shines until it appears like highly polished ebony. As the Mind becomes ever more disciplined in maturity, the "stalks" become yet more tautly and neatly woven. Both the stalks and the outer rims of the bulbous rice-like grains darken into a reddish gold colour and the entire Mind progressively changes colour, by degrees, until that part closest to the shining black base turns truly golden. The colour above it changes to a lighter brightly burnished yellow-gold and then, gradually, many beautiful shades of colour – of light blues and mauves – glow and occasionally sparkle within the golden sheen. The "sparkles" of light are emitted with energy and are themselves multi coloured. It is a truly wondrous thing to behold. No material artefact one can possibly imagine, can compare. No bejewelled tiara could ever match such beauty. The loveliest of any object of earthly nature which one could possibly conceive is as a waxen and dead thing in comparison with the living glory of a developed Mind. Moreover with that visual beauty is conveyed quality... the quality of love: love and intelligence. This is observed and known in the same way as qualities, feelings and the working of intelligence within another are conveyed to one through the human eyes.

As the Seed of Existence and the Mind further develop, that shining black base on which Mind rests becomes self-illuminated. The sheen from its ebony blackness is as a white light; and this luminous white light shines through the golden, sparkling Mind which lies atop it.

Although I have spoken of the Mind "sparkling", these "sparkles" are actually intensely bright emissions of its light.

In yet later viewings of the Mind, the ricelike grains (now of pure light) are seen to have assumed a beautiful patterned formation, the most accentuated patterning having formed around the edges or rim of its "Jewish knitted skullcap" shape and the glowing grains having assumed on its top the patterned formation of four "leaves". The entirety is still self illuminated and it still displays its constant alivedness but its colours change dependant upon the dimensional level from which it is viewed.

The deeper the Zeroness of Being attained from which Mind is viewed, so the *quality* of the Mind is perceived to be of yet more wondrous depth. Whereas there is a "buzzing" emanation of sound when it is experienced from the Stabilising dimensional viewpoint, at deeper level of Zeroness the Mind is beheld as a glorious organ of light of depthful living *Silence*.

However, from whichever level Mind is viewed, it is not seen to be in the likeness of a Lotus flower, as it has been described elsewhere. It is possible that in ancient times verbal descriptions have been given by others who have seen it but that these descriptions have been misinterpreted over the course of time by those who themselves lack direct experience. Each ricelike grain has a pointed tip as one finds on petals or leaves but they are not flat like a petal or leaf but are bulbous; and although there is a leaflike patterning on its top, as described above, the Mind cannot be likened to any blossom.

* * * *

The Body, the Mind and the Seed or Light may indeed be different facets of what we are, but they are mutually dependant and interconnected. It is a living, breathing interconnection. The concept of some religious disciplines is that the Unutterable Light (or the Brahman of Hindu terminology) within us, does not suffer. But it is our Light, the Seed of Existence within us which moves our Mind and thence the brain and body. Mind and Light together are the Observer and the Experiencer.

The Light (always in conjunction with Mind) is the experiencer of pain and joy. It is that which knows the body's hunger and thirst, that which itself hungers and thirsts for greater depth of fulfilment and freedom. The Light motivates us from a complex content of both good and evil, for the Light itself is imperfect. Therefore, as we are also motivated to action from the faults and imperfections of our own Light, we are often the cause of our own suffering. Our very Life, that Seed of our Existence, is itself evolving and needs to be yet further evolved.

As that Light develops, as its faults are transmuted and it is matured into the depths of Zeroness, it becomes a greatly enhanced, effulgent globe of Light; but it will continue to feel and suffer whilst still in the physical body. It knows the agony of violence and deprivation. It is that which motivates and propels – and that which, day by day, reaps the results of action.

IMPERFECTION

It must be patently clear to us all that we humans are imperfect beings. Each of us has faults. Some are minor, some more serious. Some of us are burdened with faults of a truly horrendous nature, such as to cause disaster to ourselves and to others.

Our faults – as well as our good characteristics and qualities – are impregnated deep within our Being. They belong to the disc of our Unutterable Light itself. This Unutterable depth – the initial creative depth of our Being before its fuller development into its deeper dimensional possibilities – is that which motivates our Stabilising internal content. And it is our Stabilising Self which in turn activates our physical behaviour and responses. You will recall that that which TAYOZAAN names the Stabilising Self (or that which is called our "Spirit" in religious terminology) is in effect the blueprint of our body. Similarly our Unutterable Light is the yet deeper internal blueprint of our Stabilising Self; and being the source of our creativity, the Unutterable is actually the level from which our destiny is directed. It is only a matter of time before that which is within our Unutterable disc of Light, both "good" and "bad", becomes manifested. It is therefore wise not to bury or be blind to our faults but to face them squarely and deal with them, for no-one else can magically clear them away for us.

Some of our imperfections we recognise and can deal with but others will remain with us to our dying day and beyond, undealt with, continuing with our Unutterable Light into our next incarnation – for we carry the essence of what we are from life to life. The fault may have become even more indelibly imprinted on our Unutterable disc of Light if we have given it free rein and allowed it to strengthen during our current incarnation. Hence the urgent importance of our gaining control and transforming the content of our creative disc during our present lifetime. We assuredly cannot escape having to face up to it at some point in our journeying. It is therefore wise not to leave it until our faults have become so entrenched that the task is the more onerous and painful.

Present-day Therapists tend to attribute blame for various psychological problems (including destructive, unsociable behaviour) on some disturbing experience which may have been suffered during our vulnerable, formative years; but the real cause may well stem from an inbuilt, already existent predisposition or fault within the person's being. Some outer circumstance or happening may well be the cause of bringing innate tendencies to the fore.

Because certain tendencies (or actual set conditions, as they may have become) such as homosexuality, or the expression of sexuality in deviant, sado-masochistic ways, are complications which are impregnated deep within the individual's Light, such preferences are felt to be "natural" and therefore completely acceptable to the person concerned. It will also be considered quite natural and therefore acceptable to those whose Light and Mind are in like condition. Even those not of similar persuasion but who wish to be sympathetic and tolerant may well agree and will argue everyone's right to freedom of expression of what is natural to them, be it a matter of sexual orientation or otherwise – with the proviso perhaps that certain constraints apply (such as only conducting certain types of behaviour in private and only sharing such practices with other consenting adults).

Those who, maybe only intuitively, recognise certain kinds of conduct to be unhealthful and/or unseemly – or to be a blatant aberration – are roundly castigated if they voice such an opinion, for as with many other imperfect behavioural tendencies in life, there is strength in numbers and because a condition of being and kind of desiring is shared by many, the belief is reinforced that it must be "normal" and should therefore be accepted. In the case of homosexuality, not only has the belief that this is a normal condition become almost cemented in some societies, it is moreover often now viewed as a condition to be actually "celebrated".

The power of mass opinion is understood and used these days increasingly effectively – and quite legitimately so when it is used to right various wrongs – but mass ignorance is a disaster to life. The human mind of the more superficial nature is strongly influenced by the views of others especially if such points of view are repeated with sufficient loudness and unity of voice, so that some instinctive evaluations which were formerly held by society at large become insidiously eroded or even eventually reversed. These days those who perceive various kinds of licentious conduct to be of a deviant, unhealthful and ignoble nature are considered unemancipated, not with the times. To voice such a view one must expect to be condemned as a straightlaced bigot of narrow view. The tables are currently turned against the defenders of healthful qualities and nobility of human conduct. One is expected to "respect" many forms of behaviour which are not worthy of respect.

Those who may or may not voice their disagreement (or actual sense of revulsion) towards various forms of deviant sexual conduct for instance, are made to feel somehow the odd ones out in modern life. They are made to feel guilty for what is interpreted as lack of broad mindedness and tolerance. With regard to the subject of homosexuality, some sit nervously on the fence, unsure what is the correct view to take of the matter. But, in fact, to do other than express one's sexuality in the male or female role according to the male or female body in which one finds oneself in this present incarnation, has been seen (with internal vision) to be both the cause and the result of a definite fault in an individual's creative disc of Light. The physical body is by nature prepared for procreative interaction between male and female. Sexual activity between man and man or woman and woman is a wasteful and sterile aberration, against nature's purpose so far as reproduction is concerned. It also involves abuse of the body. The more a person is divorced from the norm and the more he or she fulfils sexual desiring of an aberrant nature (or even desires and fantasises without action) that irregularity becomes a set feature within the individuality. The same applies to the repetition of any thought, emotion or behaviour. The pattern and quality of our thoughts, feelings and behaviour set our pathway into the future. We therefore have a strong hand in the paving of our own destinies.

The condition of homosexuality has been seen to be registered in the Stabilising dimension of the human brain as a conical section, point downwards from the centre line of the brain at the crown of the head. Whether this is at all visible as an altered state of the actual physical brain of a person of homosexual persuasion is not known by me at this time, but it is visible in the subtler Stabilising dimension of the physical body. It has become thus from a fault arising from the yet deeper creative disc of the person's Unutterable Light. The more the fault – in this instance of homosexuality – is acceded to and the more it is activated, the more rooted and developed it becomes and the less likely it is that the individual will be able to recognise it as a fault. Actually it is an illness but it will seem a natural and correct aspect of his or her nature to the individual concerned – thus causing sadness and often extreme difficulty for that person if society does not condone free expression of his or her preferred kind of sexuality. Unlike some other faults within the disc of our Light which manifest as unpleasant illnesses and which everyone will therefore, without question, definitely discern as harmful and wish to be rid of, the fault of homosexuality is associated (for those of that persuasion) with physical and emotional pleasure. It therefore holds seductive power. As relationship with another human being is involved, it also helps satisfy a natural and perfectly legitimate need for intimate closeness and companionship with another. Perhaps in some instances it holds the added attraction of enjoying "forbidden fruit" or, in the current climate of public opinion (in some countries) there is the newly found enjoyment of freedom from need for secrecy and restraint.

No doubt there will exist within many homosexual relationships a worthy depth of love. Undoubtedly there can be a sincere mutual appreciation and satisfying companionship between man and man, between woman and woman and tenderness, devotion and self sacrifice can exist between individuals of the same gender, but sexual expression is not catered for by nature between two bodies of the same sex. To subject the body to surgery to deal with this problem is a sad, desperate measure taken by some in an effort to convert themselves to their preferred gender. The body suffers mutilation but the problem is not solved. It is a very real problem, an illness, and as such should be viewed with great compassion. There is possibility of correcting this condition by means of the processes taught in the philosophy of TAYOZAAN and such help is warmly offered, with understanding, to all who may seek it.

*   *   *   *

Faults within the disc of any particular individual's Unutterable Light may involve a variety of negative tendencies or actual set negative conditions of being. The range of human negativity is wide and obviously varies from person to person. Each of us has our own content of imperfection both as to types of fault and the degree of intensity of each fault. Some kinds of fault are fairly innocuous and one may say are universal to human experience as the evolving ego is vulnerable and has its inevitable weaknesses; but some faults are so negative as to cause behaviour which brings darkness, misery and pain to others, as well as to the individual himself. We see the dark content of the human being manifesting in all societies, despoiling, harming, exploiting. There are many who vent their destructive aggression and frustrations upon others and who will go to considerable lengths and effort to cause fear and hurt, to make their negative mark upon the environment and upon society at large. In some instances, the erring individual may not appear to suffer from such negative behaviour. They may even appear to profit; but we escape nothing. As we sow, so will we assuredly reap. Our actions are our creation. And creation belongs to its creator. We are therefore attached to the darkness we inspire for it belongs to us. Conversely, we are also inseparably connected to the Light which we may engender in the course of our living, for it too belongs to us.

* * * *

Our imperfections, our weaknesses, are stimulated by the Anti-life forces (which may well have been responsible for a fault's arrival into our being in the first place). Our own Anti-Life forces activate our faults from within our own being. Our weaknesses are also targeted by the Anti-life forces outside of us in the world, particularly via the negative forces within other people.

Everyone must have experience of difficult relationships, of moods and conflicts which somehow arise, often without logical reason, despite the real wishes of the parties concerned. There is often bewildered frustration leading to anger at one's own (and the other person's) inability to understand what is happening and at our not knowing how to deal with such confused situations.

The fact and role of the Anti-life forces within life has already been more fully covered in a previous chapter; but again, from the above it is clear that each of us needs to gird our loins for a serious personal battle if our content of imprinted faults – constantly activated as it is by the negative, opposing forces – is to be overcome. Each of us is truly entrapped in our own personal condition of being. We are also locked within the conditions of life which mould our immediate environment. Although we may struggle to be independant and to live by our own intelligence and integrity, we cannot escape the mass of influence and the strong forces which impinge on us from the world at large.

The fight is real and serious; but freedom must be our aim. With benefit of a new clarity of understanding and armed with an unrelenting strength of purpose, liberation is surely possible. Courage is needed. The answer is not to rely on drugs to either suppress negative urges or give one an artificially induced boost. Stimulus or becalming induced from the outside can mostly only give superficial relief. Drugs can stimulate a kind of unnatural, temporary strength or induce a kind of temporary peace which is not truly our own. The action to produce true strength or peace needs to come from within us.

The avenue to positive, healthful change is by intelligent, rightly directed use of our own powers of Mind. This may seem simplistically obvious. It sounds fine in theory; but most of us do not know really what to do in practise.

The most valuable of educations is to learn how to develop the positive aspects of our Unutterable disc of Light and in the process gradually transform out our negativities. It is a process much akin to physics or chemistry and involves the material of Life's subtle energies.

We first need to understand our position and possibilities. There is power in intelligent understanding and however modest or limited that understanding may be in the beginning, it provides a commencing base for movement.

There are practical Systems in the philosophy of TAYOZAAN which enable us to unify and focus our energies. They show us how to clearly observe and make objective use of our content of thought and feeling. They teach us how to "feed" the Light of Life – our higher Self – with these living energies; and so develop that Seed of our Existence. We thus begin to transform our existing content.

By means of such action we begin to develop a new "I" of quality of that transformed material; a new "I" which gradually acquires its own knowledge and wisdom arising from this new direction of internal travel. We see that there is in fact something definite and positive that we can do and that provided we make the necessary effort and take the correct action, we have the means of acquiring some measure of control over our existing content. We taste the difference. The experience, the increasing understanding of the process – and the strengthening ability which comes with practise – becomes our own.

That newly developing part of our Mind has possibility of standing in freer relationship not only with our past but with our current experiencing so that, provided we make the necessary effort, there is opportunity for a different and more positive response to life than we were previously capable of.

* * * *

The objective Acceptance of TAYOZAAN is a definite internal movement effected by the Mind. Such Acceptance without rejection does not mean that discrimination is absent. On the contrary, one's powers of discrimination become greatly intensified. We then find ourselves with possibility of acting from a different level of awareness than we previously possessed. Such discriminatory intelligence becomes ever more subtle as one progresses and we become more aware and are gradually freed from our past conditioning.

So we see that we do have the means of acquiring greater mastery over our Mind and emotions and over those experiences which newly enter our day to day living, for those new experiences need no longer be received by and responded to from the conditioned maze of our old content. Gradually, as we form a new relationship with ourselves, as we begin to free ourselves from the mould of our past and produce a new content, we find the possibility of acting from that new content.

* * * *

By means of acts of conscious Acceptance into our internal Light, all that energy, that material of our living state, is utilised to produce a deeper dimensional quality of our Being. It produces a new and increasingly emancipated intelligence and enhanced awareness from which to function. This action of Acceptance, as it is understood and applied in TAYOZAAN, is a science. It is also an art, for the action simultaneously involves bringing into play, and thereby developing, the nobler human qualities of feeling.

The action of Mind which is the Acceptance of which I speak, acts as a nutrient, initially in the development of one's Unutterable level of Being. And as the Unutterable light is matured, there begins to be produced within its depth "substance" of the Non Existent dimensional nature. An internal momentum is engendered which progresses subtly yet assuredly yet further into the eternal depths... into a finer, more intensified Eternal Zeroness, into that living "Nothingness", that Timeless dimension which can never be filled for it is without boundaries; limitless.

One's Light, one's Seed of Existence, can therefore progressively achieve a Selfhood of an ever more internally/eternally evolving nature. External evolution continues but the outward dissipation of one's life now takes a more definite turn inwards, to consciously co-operate with the cosmic internal/eternal evolutionary flow: in tune with the inward breath of the Body of Life. There is no doubt within the individual that one is now marching in this direction. One knows when one is acquiring or has acquired a new and qualitied inner substance of Being. One knows when one's outlook on life, quality of motivation and purpose has changed. One knows when one's priorities, when one's sense of what is important have become differently oriented. And one knows that with such knowledge comes responsibility.

We are each of us responsible for our own lives; and it is impossible to opt out. We can do nothing other than go forward when we understand that we cannot escape ourselves but that we will continue to be, for we are Life and Life is indestructible.

* * * *

The Seed of Existence, the Light which is the real "Self" of each one of us, is at varyingly different stages of development from person to person. Our capacity and will for change varies from person to person as does the amount of effort which an individual may make at different stages of his or her existence. Therefore, when we speak of our "true Self", that is only the highest point of development a person's Light may have attained at any given point in Time in the long course of that being's evolution.

This position of reality – that is what we are at this point in Time – must be held in context of what may yet be possible of achievement. It must be held in context of what still lies within our destiny. Seen from the point of view that we are all at different stages of evolution and are, each of us, at different levels of maturity – right from the point of each rebirth into the manifest world – it is not true to say that all men are born equal. The circumstance of life into which we may be reincarnated, the possibilities which may open to us, our abilities and what we may make of them, all vary enormously, so that we are certainly not all equal in that regard either. But we all originated from, belong to and are *of* All Life. We are all part of this great and complex Process of Life with its enormous range of possibilities. And we all, inescapably, belong to the ultimate Destiny of the Allness. In that sense we are all equal.

* * * *

Mind serves higher Mind; hence we refer in TAYOZAAN to "serving" the Seed of our Existence. No-one can perform this act for you. Each person must make his or her own effort, but another who already has experience and growth can instruct, guide and encourage.

Anyone can always help by stimulating the positive within another. Like attracts like. A word or act of love, understanding or compassion has its own life, its own vibration or quality of energy which can touch that of like nature within another. A sincere blessing can therefore enhance the positive Light within the being of another person. A blessing of high intensity from the quality of a developed Light is an effective act. It has power. As has been previously stated, the qualitatively charged blessing of a highly evolved Being who is matured into the eternal dimensions can cause new creation within the Cosmos. Such an action which effects a Beginning of new worlds can be termed an act of cosmic procreation. And even in its greatly less matured state, our Unutterable Light reflects, albeit microcosmically, that Unutterable creative level which is the source of manifest Existence. But, of course, the degree and scale of creativity possible to a Supreme Being bears little comparison to the creative capacity of a relatively undeveloped mortal.

* * * *

As the Unutterable Light develops and there begins to be produced within its depth substance of the Non Existent eternal nature, our Unutterable Light can gradually be cleansed of its imprint of faults and be fully transmuted into a Selfhood of Non Existent dimensional quality. By the continued efforts of the dedicated, it is possible to further evolve into yet higher qualitied states of eternal

Zeroness until there is complete fusion with the Wholeness. An incomparable chord of Oneness is struck when an individual becomes a Completed Self within the Unfathomable depths of the Zahtaum Zeroness of Love.

A vitally necessary and interlinked strand of action in that development of our Light is that which overcomes the Anti Life force of opposition and which cleanses our Light of its imperfections and larger faults. As has been clarified, Anti Life is inherent within the very substance of Existence, it being within the initial act of creation. Imperfection is therefore within the very nature of the Unutterable dimension from which Existence sprang.

Whenever the Unutterable moves there is a creative action which bears its own Anti Life content within it. And so "matter" – and therefore all life forms within the manifest world – has Anti Life opposition inherently within it. Similarly, perforce, we ourselves continue to create Anti Life force by our living actions no matter how nicely and carefully we may live. In fact the more strong our Unutterable Light becomes, the more powerful will be its creativity and the more potent therefore will be the Anti Life opposition which that creative force engenders. Every action we take, every thought that is formulated or spoken, every emission of emotion that comes from us, is a form of creative activity, however weak. The stronger the action, thought or feeling – be it of "negative" or "positive" quality – involves a corresponding Anti Life force of opposition by way of counterbalance. Measure to measure; force to force.

Anti Life opposition is therefore a natural phenomenon. It is as an anchor which restrains, a weight and a power which impells us outward and downward into the grosser world. It is an impediment but also the friction which bestirs; that which agitates and thereby causes what would otherwise stagnate to move and change. However, Anti Life opposition resulting from a nobly inspired thought or feeling is not so laden with Anti Life force as are thoughts, feelings and actions which actually originate from our base Anti Life Self, the gross content of our Being.

Those who at least to some extent recognise and acknowledge their own Anti Life content (we are more likely to see it within others) and who wish to free themselves from the burden of its disruptive, painful influence, are already poised for action. It is appreciated that something needs to be done. Control is desired, we wish to change our condition but we have little idea how to achieve mastery over the forces which oppose us. If we do try to effect change we usually find it to be a losing battle, locked as we normally are within our weak condition, dominated by much stronger forces than we have the vision or strength to deal with.

Many just do not see the need for change. They do not, therefore, seek liberation and are certainly not interested enough to make any effort themselves to better their situation. Their Anti Life content will of course vigorously oppose any move to lessen its power. It will oppose the awakening of intelligence and will particularly oppose the taking of any action which will lead to the weakening of its domination or to its actual annihilation. And our established Anti Life thinking and feeling processes will present all manner of excuses, inducing a state of lethargy and procrastination to offput the commencement of any such action.

When really threatened by one's higher Self's struggle to obtain liberation from its dominating influence, our

Anti Life content will fight back. Its nature is challenging and antagonistic, especially towards others. It will activate inner conflict, causing emotional confusion – especially doubt – so that the individual may well lose emotional control, becoming angry and aggressively rejecting. Our Anti-life content locks us in a prison of ignorance and stagnation from which it is indeed difficult to escape. A pall of inertia and disinterest shrouds our internal Light from seeing its own condition. When we have seen and understood this, we see that repetitive effort is needed to disperse that cloud of ignorant unconcern which habitually descends upon us and masks our internal Light whenever we become spiritually inactive.

We have to repeatedly work as it were against a natural gravitational downward pull upon our internal Light. We have to constantly make effort to reawaken and combat the magnetically seductive pull of the finite world of matter and that of the gross Anti Life field of Existence. These two levels or aspects of our experiencing: the outer World of the Brimonda and our Anti Life Self (connected as it is with the Anti Life forces within the Brimonda and within the internal dimensions) are respectively our Seventh and Eighth levels of Selfhood. These grossest levels are of the ITNESS. They are a vital and integral part of the nature of the whole Life Process to which we belong.

We must awaken and resist the force of this natural downward and outward tide of Life. Such effort produces a "turning about" within which enables one to move inwards and upwards, newly directed. Intentional, conscious action is required. It is a new ball game but an immensely rewarding and adventurous one which is itself an aspect of that ITNESS: the Life Process. It is that aspect of the Life Process which belongs to the more consciously functioning levels of Creation. So, let us make positive use of Life's opposition, for the effort of overcoming is an enormous aid to movement in our ascension upon the Zero dimensional ladder. In fact Life's opposition provides the only means whereby the Light of Life can be built, refined and strengthened. Life's opposing forces enable Life itself to attain its ultimate purpose.

* * * *

The Anti Life Self will deny that there is any real problem. It will not want to allow us to admit to possessing such a degree of imperfection that it actually needs to be dealt with. One's negative ego is offended, deflated, to be adjudged imperfect. If pressured by another or challenged by one's own higher reasoning, the force of Anti Life incites a flare-up of irritability. The Anti Life Self wants to be left alone, to be allowed to retain its power, to have freedom to increase and expand its domination. Therefore the position remains that most of us will not agree to bestir ourselves to take any action whatsoever to change our state of being, great though our need may be. Many will profess interest, may read many books, paying lip service to spiritual endeavour, toying with this or that discipline, but will not genuinely seek change, for in general we are neither prepared to make the necessary effort nor do we have the courage to face ourselves. We can liken the position to that of a starving degenerate covered in dirt and slime (for that, shocking though the truth may be, is our internal condition before we work to uplift and cleanse it) but who yet denies having need of food or that there can be any benefit in taking a bath. Until we have actually eaten and been strengthened, until we have allowed our body into the cleansing balm of water, we will not know the joy of refreshment and good health. We will remain not knowing how improved our whole condition could be.

Our lives will continue to remain unsatisfyingly unfulfilled, by reason of our own default.

Similarly, those of us who are unaware of the higher states of being it is possible for us to enjoy will yet nevertheless argue in denial of the existence of any such higher state merely because it is unknown to their experience; and the offered outstretched hand of help will be ignored, or refused. Sometimes this refusal of help stems from sheer reluctance to admit one's own ignorance and need, especially when the ego has false illusions of its own superiority and fears revealing itself to others. There is also one's own fear of oneself. There is the fear, in facing oneself, of what one may find.

The Anti-life force which is within us, that which is within the physical world and that which is within each level of the Zero worlds, has cunning and the advantage of foreknowledge. It is therefore swift in countering instruction or movement inspired from the eternal Light within. It will pre-empt any action likely to oppose it. Therefore it is very difficult initially to touch a person's Unutterable Self to inspire the way to change. The Stabilising Self standing mid-way, serves as a bridge between the Unutterable Light and the gross Anti-life Self. The Stabilising Self, the internal personality, does in fact on occasions muster sufficient discernment and discrimination to see what is besetting it and knows it has a measure of choice but it will tend to take what appears to be the easiest way out and will mostly allow negativity to reign. To elect, by sheer default, to maintain an ignorant posture of attitude or behaviour may seem the easiest way but it is merely the laziest choice. The fruit of such choice is the continuing pain of our faults and an ever strengthening bondage to the Anti-life forces.The stubborn pay a high price and reap the hardest result in the end.

* * * *

It is a question of exposure of Self to intelligent Self with a stance of objective acceptance. Mind and Light develop Mind and Light. In this way Light increases its creative intelligence. Such facing up and exposure leaves us neither crushed nor vacant when we understand that there is action to be taken which truly achieves; for not only is there the means for obtaining liberation but we find that the cleansed void with which we are left is in fact our own freed inner space which is now possessed by one's own eternal Light. That which is one's real identity now possesses its own domain and is freer to expand into yet higher dimensional zones.

It is most fulfilling to move towards achieving and functioning from the integrity of one's higher Self. There is deep satisfaction in the gradual attainment of increased knowledge and wisdom and in the blossoming of our capacity for love and compassion. There is immense comfort in experiencing one's truer identity and in moving ever further towards an identity of increasing quality. It can be likened to discovering and gradually coming into possession of our internal Home where we truly belong; a place within where we feel quietly strong and are at peace, for there we are unified... there is no division, no duality between the Timed and the Timeless. It is a place where the chord struck is a total YES of affirmation. That Home is our Self.

* * * *

We each have an inner and an outer destiny. Development of the nature of which I speak influences and directs both. Each day that we live presents opportunity for, as it were, putting something in the Bank in both directions. Both directions call for evolutionary maturity and fulfilment. Both our internal and external destinies are, therefore, important. It is vital that we find and manifest the right balance of interest and endeavour towards both the outer and the inner, for in truth the physical worlds and the Zero worlds are only different aspects of but one Reality. And that Oneness of Reality must move in a healthful balance of growth towards its ultimate Completion.

Some cultures place too much emphasis on one or the other aspect of Life. Those who do not value the external reality make little or no effort towards outer existence and a range of impoverishment is the visible outcome. However, conversely, much of the world is almost entirely engrossed in matters of material value, plunged headlong into external existence with little thought of there being any deeper reason or purpose for our being alive. In fact the majority of us seldom, if ever, question even the extraordinary and mysterious phenomenon of our very existence. When the internal reality is not consciously sought, the evolutionary process will continue to be long and slow, progressing mostly mechanically. In fact as the interest and desires of such individuals are focused solely on the material world, they will feel repetitively drawn to the manifest level where they feel most at home, despite the inherent harshness of existence which each rebirth entails. In such cases many further incarnations must, of necessity, be borne.

To work towards one's own internal development may seem to some to smack of self-interest, to be a selfish pursuit – but whatever we achieve towards elevating our own Being will, inevitably, benefit the totality; for all and everything, both large and small moves towards a mutual destiny, every particle of Life being inseparable from and therefore contributing to Itself in its entirety.

* * * *

Contrary to the commonly held concepts: first that we originate from a supreme Perfection – in the belief that the Beginning of Beginnings or the initial Cause of all Causes is the one all-perfect "Godhead" – and secondly that we merely need to find and return to that perfect Beginning, we see that in reality the Beginning is neither perfect nor matured. Therefore to return to the very Beginning would be like returning to the womb. In fact it would be akin to returning to pre embryonic state.

Being neither perfect nor matured, we see that all that which originates from First Beginning has yet to fully Become. First Beginning is in process of Becoming. It has to achieve that which is within its own blueprint of all blueprints of possibility; and we ourselves are part of, are within that maturing Process. You and I and all Life are, therefore, also inseparable from the glorious Purpose and destined End of that original imperfection.

Therefore, in speaking of man's imperfections, we cannot – nor do we – here stand on a pedestal nor point a condemnatory finger at anyone. The burden of imperfection is common to us all.

In the lowest wrong – and of the highest good – I claim a connection as man the spiritual animal: the ITNESS, the EVER IS Gem.

FALSE GODS, PRAYER AND SUBMISSION

Modern technology has given us modes of transportion and methods of communication light years in advance of that which existed but a few years ago. The world has opened up to the masses in a quite extraordinary way and with quite astonishing speed; so that we, the ordinary man in the street, are today possessed of knowledge of our world to an extent rarely enjoyed even by the privileged few whose education had previously made them privy to more knowledge than most and whose wealth permitted a more widely travelled life style. What is occurring in other countries, how other peoples live and view life, their beliefs and ideologies have become virtually common knowledge... knowledge imparted to us in a constant flow of information through the media. And, for increasing numbers, such increased knowledge is now gained by direct observation, international travel having become almost commonplace for many ordinary folk of relatively modest means.

As we know, prior to this great "opening up" of communication which has brought us into incomparably closer contact with each other than ever before, the peoples of this planet lived in fairly insular groupings, each grouping having established its own set of beliefs: beliefs and ritualistic behaviours based mostly on mythological and/or religious concepts which, historically, have undergone change or modification by reason of the effects of periodic migrations, acts of conquest or the influence of missionary zeal.

All life feels its vulnerability. Just to be alive in this world inevitably presents us with pressures and difficulties. The whole unrelenting task of mere survival is harsh for most creatures. By necessity every living creature is a predator existing at the expense of other life; for every life form requires food and all food is another form of life of some kind or the other. It is a process involving constant struggle and uncertainty; one of pain and death. Yet, on the plus side, Life also expresses through Nature its more easily acceptable face in the wonders of its majestic, awesome might together with its many shades of beauty, exquisite delicacies and fragilities. Life amazes us with its astoundingly intricate interplay of intelligence which is constantly at work throughout manifestation.

From we humans' point of view "Life" itself is miraculous. The fact that there is Life at all is surely the greatest mystery. The human being is apparently the only sufficiently evolved life form on this planet to question the fact of our existence but although this mystery has been probed and questioned by humanity over the course of thousands of years, so much still remains unknown – and seemingly unknowable.

Clearly we are all here, experiencing existence and, clearly, we are at the mercy of immensely more powerful forces than our own. Therefore the fact that we have instinctively feared, and had sense of awe and reverence towards both the enormity of the world in which we find ourselves and its powers, both tangible and invisible, is hardly surprising.

The forces of Nature have been obvious objects for our awed respect and fear. It is a very narrow margin of balance on which we depend for our mere survival on this Earth. We are dependant upon Nature's controlled restraint and beneficence even more acutely if we are, moreover, to actually flourish. We are so fragile, so easily crushed by Nature's might and completely dependant upon her sustenance, for no matter what efforts we ourselves may make, we need the raw materials of Nature with which to work. We are intricately and inescapably interwoven with her great Process.

It is equally understandable that mountains and rivers have engendered a sense of the ancient and the mystical; also that forests, or specific trees or animals, have assumed special significance to those whose lives they closely affect. It is therefore not surprising that such objects of Nature have come to be venerated and believed to be possessed of spiritual powers. So it is really only natural that there came to be belief (as indeed still exists to this day) in Nature Gods in the form of the elements, the sun, the moon or whatever else may have assumed special significance to the human being. And humankind has for millenia responded to that which it has elevated to such special status by making obeisance to it – obeisance not just of a respectful or reverential nature but obeisance in attitude of subjection. But by this stance of subjection, or subjugation, mankind sacrifices the dignity of his own innate nobility. By developing an attitude of subjugation man denies himself the self respect of acting from his own intelligence and higher principles, so allowing confidence in his own conscience to be undermined.

This inner posture of subjection, or subjugation, causes a large portion of humanity to continue following the ignorances of tradition which require him to behave in ways quite unacceptable to higher intelligence. Incredibly man still, to this day, makes blood sacrifices to his chosen deity to appease or placate, to support pleas for favours or by way of thanksgiving. Countless sacrifices have been made to Gods at countless altars throughout the centuries. How many millions still make offerings at shrines throughout the planet, not seeing that this is akin to offering a millionaire his own possessions by way of gift. It is akin to offering a wealthy man food from his own kitchen, proferring him flowers cut from his own garden and telling him "Here too is one of your sheep which I have slaughtered for you... so now, as I have been so generous, please reward me by giving me what I want". And when, moreover, the offering involves the pain and bloodshed of a living creature in the sacrifice of its life, would not anyone of normal, healthful heart and mind adjudge someone behaving in this way to be in need of mental care and education? Yet such conduct is not regarded as abnormal by many millions of otherwise relatively normal people even now in this supposedly greatly more enlightened age.

A whole plethora of manmade mythology and superstition has arisen around the numerous pagan beliefs which abound on this Earth; as it has similarly arisen around what religions view as the more advanced concept of there being but one "*super*natural", all-embracing and invisible Godhead. But the linchpin of belief continues to be worship based on an attitude of *subjection*. Religions continue to instill in mankind this need to worship, this need to beg and plead in prayer in attitude of prostrating both body and inner being to "God" in abasement, with conviction of one's inborn sinfulness and inferiority. Religions still reinforce this mould, forever urging abject remorse for one's "sins", perpetuating a burdensome sense of guilt which has long served as a millstone weighing down the human soul.

Religions moreover still perpetuate belief in our complete dependancy upon God as the only means of obtaining pardon and merciful absolution for our sinful state. We are even taught dependancy on God for the granting – also by way of merciful gift – of the *qualities* we lack. We are led to pray for goodness as well as for the provision of our other needs.

Religion continues to instill in us through prayer and rituals the apparent need of God to be continually praised and glorified.

The more wholly the adherent embodies this entire mental, emotional and behavioural posture required by religion, the more successful is it believed he will be in obtaining celestial favour – and the more sincere and pious is he considered to be.

* * * *

The great welter of mythology, fable, and stories *of mankind's own creation* which abound on this Earth have become imbued with a mystical quality, and so are held to be beyond question, as if the Truth be mysteriously within the words, thus taking them outside any need to comply with reason, common sense – or reality. A large part of Hinduism comprises mythology and fable which defy either logical reasoning or the known facts of life and which therefore require imaginative interpretation in attempt to make any acceptable sense of them; yet such literature is still believed – and held in high regard even by the educated. One can only wonder whether these tales were in fact meant for the serious seeker or whether they originated as fairy tales for children which here and there can be seen to carry a moral message.

As is the case with much of the literature of the world religions, there is little or no real clarity of instruction, no real help in these writings to aid spiritual progress. In fact they are prone to convey confused and contradictory messages which are far from helpful. Even those perhaps previously cherished works of literature, which have been held in high regard by seekers of truth the world over as our main source of esoteric knowledge, are actually sadly lacking; of no real practical help at the end of the day. For even though they have power to inspire and cause one to be moved by their sheer poetry of expression, one comes eventually to the reluctant conclusion that such literature is full of ambiguity (or actual contradiction), slipping and sliding this way and that, speaking in riddles or parables requiring interpretation and yet further interpretation; finally leaving one feeling sadly confused – or even cruelly betrayed – and little or none the wiser.

Under pressure of the power of traditional thought and longstanding influence, there are many who, even with benefit of far broader knowledge than our forebears enjoyed, still turn a blind eye to what they must surely see as the clearly archaic and unsatisfactory content of the religious literature on which the various World faiths are founded. How must the scientists, astronomers and anthropologists of today view the cosmology of the Old Testament of the Bible with its simplistic pronouncements concerning creation and the arrival of life on Earth? Although it is supposedly a work of divine revelation from an Allknowing, omniscient Creator, the writers of that long saga portrayed a strangely limited view of reality. There is no revelation as to the magnitude of the cosmos in terms of its vastness or the enormity of its timescale nor does it educate us to understand that this small planet Earth is but a miniscule part of that vast creation. Even viewed from our present knowledge, still incomplete though it be, the biblical expanation of creation is (to put it mildly) childishly inadequate.

Moreover, this supposedly divine revelation offers no reason for creation. No depth of purpose for existence is revealed to a mankind long hungering and thirsting for understanding and real guidance to inspire intelligent co-operation. What a missed opportunity.

And what a poor example mankind is set by the reasoning, behaviour and demands of a God who reveals itself to be not only cruel and vindictive but jealous, capricious and unjust. The God of the Old Testament of the Bible is in fact shown to be a murderous tyrant, of such character as to dismay and shock the sensibilities of any ordinary decent hearted mere mortal. How can it be that the standards aspired to by many ordinary sensitive creatures of creation are higher than that of the Creator? But as that "holy" book tells us, this is a God who, inexplicably, has made constant demand that blood sacrifice of his own creation be made to him for his glorification...the killing and offering up to him of creatures which, if he in truth be our Creator, already were his; were already part of his "living" glory. This is a God who expressed pleasure, the Bible tells us, in the very odour of such burnt flesh offerings. He is a God who hardened the hearts of man to perform acts of "disobedience" and then sadistically meted punishment, not only to the offenders but to whole tribes of innocent people, to their children and to their children's children into succeeding generations. And as if that were not unjust enough, for good measure he decreed devastation upon the Earth by pestilence and famine, bringing misery and premature annihilation to vegetion and animal life quite innocent of the "crime" he adjudged had been committed .... acts of a purportedly loving, merciful "Father" of unbelievably wanton destruction and cruelty; acts perpetrated by this God upon his creation in state of vengeful wrath.

The Book of Revelation of that "holy" work almost runs out of horrible ideas for the final extermination of life on Earth but each pestilence, disease or act of ruthless savagery never it seems will be allowed to swiftly obliterate all life. Presumably that would spoil God's sadistic pleasure – just as a cat wishes to gain utmost satisfaction from its prey before it expires. How is it that a Creator who caused Life to be would not have power to simply withdraw the life element from his creation should he wish to do so, painlessly and mercifully?

Despite poverty and his never ceasing struggle for survival, man has also been required to give much of the little he has to build opulent Temples to glorify this demonic natured entity. Man was commanded to continue to make ritualistic blood sacrifice, to offer up the fruits of his labours and continue to show unceasing adulation to appease this despot's wrath and curry his favours. And this is the Jehovah still worshipped to the present day. This is the God of the Jews. This is the God of Christ. For the New Testament of the Christian faith is founded on the belief that Christ was the son of God – and it is made clear in Christ's teachings that his God was the God of the Old Testament of the Bible.

Similar requirement is made by the Gods of the Muslim and Hindu faiths for man's subjection, prayers and constant adulation but, were the God of any religion in truth a Supreme Being and the Creator of this world, being already possessed of all the treasures of Life he would have no such vain requirements. A true Supreme Being neither demands, wants nor needs any creature's worship. Our own Himmonda truly does not wish it. In revealing contrast, the "holy" books of religions, the Bible and the Koran in particular, instill in us the need to repetitively assert how all glorious, all powerful and all merciful be their Gods whilst, in the next breath, the same God promises tortuous and never ending punishment to be the fate of those whom he may adjudge guilty of some failure, be the failure merely that of unbelief; the qualities actually possessed by the unbeliever and the leading of a good life seemingly not counting or deemed to be as important as meeting the arbitrary laws and demands of religion. This neither accords with love, mercy nor justice.

In chapter after chapter of the Old Testament of the Bible, Jehovah is depicted as a jealous, ruthless despot, one who inspires and incites mankind to warfare, to commit acts of incredible violence and cruelty, encouraging pogroms and ravages of destruction resulting in "nothing being left that breathed": an elitist, petty God who actually encourages his chosen people to obtain gain by conquest, promising he will accord them victory... at price of their eschewing allegiance to any other God but agreeing to obey his commands and to worship him alone in complete subjection to his will.

Adherents of the Muslim faith are similarly enjoined to surrender their human will to the will of God; in fact to become "slaves" of Allah.

The concept of religion is that the more total be the surrender of one's will to God the better. The no doubt sincere belief and hope of the religious is that a more perfect will than their own, in fact the holiest of Wills, will come to motivate and transform their lives.

Followers of the Hindu faith are taught to abandon the world, to treat this manifest experience as illusory and to immerse themselves in Krishna, in Ram or in Brahma; again the emphasis being on the surrender of one's own will to that of "God".

Although it would appear that Gautama Buddha reached the understanding that there is no Being or God to be worshipped or to whom one should pray, it is evident that there are thousands of Buddhists in various regions of the world who rely strongly on prayer and worship as the mainstay of their religious expression. However it is my strong conviction that the Buddha indeed achieved a Zero dimensional level of Being. In my view Gautama Buddha attained state of maturity way beyond his time. Standing alone he showed enormous courage in voicing what must have been statements of the most controversial, nay earthshaking nature, so far as the religious establishments of his day were concerned. Right up to the present time I do not believe there can be many who know what it was he came to experience. I have the deepest respect with all the love of my heart for this great Being.

* * * *

Sadly, mankind is seriously misdirected – and in so many ways. When the eyes are opened this fact will be seen; it will become transparently obvious.

Any entity which requires a Being to surrender his or her will to it, shows itself to be of Anti Life nature. Any entity which requires glorification and our prayers, similarly reveals itself to be a force of that gross level; and those who encourage others to follow this demeaning stance of obeisance and dependancy, devout and sincere though they may be, unwittingly act as agent to those forces which keep mankind from knowing and coming into possession of its true heritage.

Entities of Anti Life force nature prey on and sap our emotional and mental energies. Millions of souls pour out their energies in prayer and adulation, not realising that in doing so they fuel, feed and empower the Anti Life field of existence.

Certainly any entity which instructs its adherents to kill or maim, to stone or amputate the limbs of any creature as punishment for wrongdoing – or cause pain or harm to any life form – confirms its demonic nature. Yet, extraordinarily, despite there being so much of the demonic staring us in the face, whether they be "real" forces of other-dimensional nature which manipulate mankind, or whether they be merely figments of mankind's imagination which over the course of time have become cemented into a form of mystic reality – these entities, these "Gods", are reverenced as Gods of Love, Mercy and Compassion even though there is so much evidence to the contrary.

Whilst it is true that within the books of religion there are exhortations to goodness and some commendable instruction and advice is given, betwixt the statements of kindness and mercy and the assurances of love, there remains an enormous amount which shouts to the contrary. And there is the constant wielding of a big stick... a threatening stick forever poised in striking position. Fear keeps mankind under control and fear is the insidious weapon of religions. This fear is kept perennially alive by repeated threats of harsh retribution, doom and hellfire should man fail to toe the line and meet religion's demands.

Humankind is also kept bowed and well "in its place" under a yoke of guilt. We are constantly reminded of our innate "sinfulness", of our total dependancy upon God for salvation and forgiveness. Religions have imposed over humanity a forbidding cloud of apprehension, a fear of judgmental rejection which is deeply imprinted within our psyche.

We are born into a longstanding set of superstitious and truly harmful beliefs which most of us accept almost without question – especially when those of seemingly superior status and intellect have believed and continue to believe in them. We are easily influenced, easily captivated by mass belief and opinion. The psyche becomes "hooked" and once hooked it generally remains compliant. Even if one decides to be freeminded, to make one's own discriminatory choices and no longer be shunted along the tracks of traditional outlook or current viewpoint, we willy nilly remain affected for it is most difficult to break free from that which is ingrained within or imposed upon our psyche. And the mental and emotional influence of religious dogma and belief is deeply entrenched.

To follow the masses, to continue to agree with all that which is the accepted viewpoint of our community and has become our way of life, presents the seemingly most easy, trouble-free way in which to continue to exist. Belonging to a community gives us sense of security. To participate in shared activities and comfortingly familiar rituals, provides structure to our lives. It all constitutes the "culture" to which one belongs. Our culture is a structure providing forms of support and enjoyment without which many would feel quite bereft. The old and the familiar are powerfully influential, providing sense of stability and continuity. Anything which uproots or threatens to uproot us from the seemingly safe anchorage of the familiar, ruffles our feathers. We feel actually threatened. Therefore that which is established and familiar continues to be cherished and protected – often fiercely so – even if on closer scrutiny such an attitude and that which we are protecting goes against all logical sense and even against moral principle.

If one is prepared to begin the task of freeing oneself from all this conditioning and make effort to live from a freer, more sincere intelligence of being, just ask yourself when next you pray: What am I doing?" and "To what exactly am I submitting my will?" Such questions do not normally even get to be thought let alone actually asked. So much do we blindly accept.

The stark fact of the matter is that most of humankind remains as it were hypnotised, under the spell of set acceptances and dogma born out of centuries of influence and manipulation. But Truth is to be sought within the human's own Being. It is achieved *by and for* that Light of Life which is within the depth of each person. That is the direction in which we, each of us, need to point our aspirations and sincere endeavours of heart and Mind.

The human needs to achieve glorification of that Life which is his own internal Light. It is his own responsibility to evolve his own Light. For this he needs to employ his own strengths and to mature his own noble qualities. He needs to use his own intelligence to obtain ever increasing depths of understanding and wisdom. For he must become possessed of Truth which is truly his own; Truth which cannot be taken away or removed from him because it becomes the very *nature* of his own Being.

One cannot obtain Truth by begging for it. On the contrary, the more man prays and begs something else for that which he himself should rise up and achieve for himself, the more weakened and misled become his precious instruments of accomplishment: the human will, intelligence and force of desire.

We need to increasingly refine and strengthen those vital attributes of our Will, higher intelligence and force of desire. "Desire" here refers to the motivating force of passion which comes from a developing nobility of heart. Desire, when connected with an increasingly refined intelligence and Willpower, energises the forwarding of our growth. In contrast, the more humankind prays and begs from a stance of passivity and weakness and the more we waste the sincere love of our yearning hearts in wrong direction, the more imprisoned we become and the more vulnerable we are to Life's opposition: the Anti Life entities and their forces.

Prayer will not place even a spoonful of rice into the mouths of the hungry. We have to make the necessary effort to put it there. Neither can, nor therefore, will goodness ever be handed to us on a plate. *We* have to *move*, to make effort to change. One would think this an obvious fact of life but yet again, strangely, we do not see that which actually stares us in the face.

In fact submission of one's Will is highly dangerous. A combined stance of submission and prayer offers the perfect entre for the Anti Life forces. The vultures are forever vigilant for prey, forever waiting to pounce on the vulnerable and the weak. The shocking reality is that by his begging stance and relinquishment of his Will (that divine attribute of his very Life) *mankind is worshipping and offering himself to the forces of Anti Life*. No wonder that humankind on this Earth is relentlessly expressing the nature of Anti Life in a continuing hellish vortex of destructive behaviour. Mankind seems incapable of co-existing in harmony for any length of time. Antipathy is rife. Without cessation, warfare is ensuing somewhere on Earth. Rejection, expressed at varying levels of intensity, seems to be endemic within human nature. Vicious acts of torture and other gross atrocities abound. No race or country on this Earth can be hailed as having a history free from the blight of inhumanity in expressions of hatred, violence and injustice.

Apart from human manipulation and exploitation of his own kind, there is a neverending greedy ravaging of the planet itself and man's ruthless exploitation of other life forms wherever gain can be seized.

Although, thankfully, on the overall canvas of existence there is much to be seen of the other, compensatingly acceptable and beauteous face of humanity, we seem to be locked into an apparently inescapable downward spiral of negativity. Clearly religions have not provided the way to change the world for the better, otherwise history and our present situation would not be as they are. In fact religions have themselves been the root and cause of much misery and, indeed, of horrendous, blatant evil. This sorry indictment applies not only to the past but to the present time.

Religions not only fail us by ignorance of the correct route to spiritual emancipation and advancement but they point us in a totally wrong direction. The falsehood and deception of that wrong direction keeps humankind in ignorance of the meaning and purpose of Life. Religions therefore stand in the way of our real education: that depthful, truly purposeful education which should bring us to an understanding of how each of us can fulfil not only that which is our destiny but that which is our very obligation to Life.

* * * *

Neither the Jews nor any other section of humanity has a Creator special to them. There is no chosen race. Were it so it would be an enormity of injustice.

The "justice" of the Old Testament of the Bible taught "An eye for an eye; a tooth for a tooth". The New Testament tells us that Jesus Christ refuted that teaching with "But I say unto you..." and he preached forgiveness and love. The Christian Church does not accuse Christ of heresy or blasphemy by reason of his contradiction of the authority of the Old Testament. His contradiction has won support as being superior teaching, according with the more evolved and enlightened consciousness and conscience of later times. (Nonetheless Christ acknowledged Jehovah, that God of the Old Testament – despite all his horrendously demonic ways – to be his God, his heavenly Father and no explanation was proferred concerning this previously given, highly questionable advice).

There is spiritual evolution as well as evolution of the physical world of matter. Therefore let us get up off our knees and see all that unseemly prostration and empty, unproductive incantation for what it is! Let us stand on our own two legs, in calm and dignified possession of our own individually unique Beings, no longer slave to the forces of Anti Life. Let us straighten our spines with a quiet current of noble intent and in spirit of love, gratitude and sincerity have self respect. Be grateful for our bodies. Care for the body – this extraordinarily wonderful living mechanism – and appreciate all its faculties and powers. Let us afford the same quality of respect to others – and be prepared to take a new, totally honest look at Life, even if such honest reappraisal be painful.

Have faith in eternal Truth. As with commencing any form of education, one has to have faith that there is something to be learnt. One does not become Master of a subject without going through a process of learning. Even though we may only be able to take one baby step at a time, let us therefore quest from and build our own depth of intelligence and then have the courage to stand by the convictions of our new evaluations... whilst being prepared to move on to yet further re-evaluation as we travel up and forward into fuller and ever subtler understanding. Therefore that which strikes note of Truth within you, uphold without fear. Make that Truth your own. But never close the door in the belief that one has finally "arrived", for there will assuredly be yet further depths of wisdom to achieve as one continues the journey ever onward into the eternal.

Have confidence in the fact that the intelligent Mind rests on a very creative source: the Light of Life within us; and it is the combined action of both of these aspects of our Selfhood (the Mind and its Light) which enables us to transform our old content and build a Self of a truly higher substance of Being. As one begins to build, culture and further cultivate that creative higher substance of Being it will be found that one's creative source is now so activated that there is no end to further inspiration; no end to further progress. And you will know for yourself that, at last, you have found the correct, effective way forward.

* * * *

The Himmondas do not seek nor do they need praise. They do not require our worship nor to be served. No Supreme Being in the Cosmos (of which there are millions) would make such demand.

Just imagine how it would be if one were perpetually assailed by billions of pleas, by whingings, by torments of mind and emotion... being begged night and day for forgiveness, and/or for various other gifts and favours. Imagine having projected towards one an unceasing barrage of words repetitively, and mostly emptily, voiced. Even to be subjected to a never ending torrent of praise would assuredly be a burden needing to be borne, not enjoyed. Only some entity of the nature of Anti Life would want and benefit from these energies, sapped from the living manifest world. I speak from experience. I have actually seen Anti Life entities swell in girth and power when given love.

It is a great mistake to empower Anti Life. In doing so mankind makes ever larger and heavier rod for its own back. Therefore, know that the "Gods" of any religion who seek to be worshipped – whether they bear such exalted names as "Jehovah", "Allah" or any other perhaps long cherished and respected title – are of Anti Life force nature: *the basest strata of Life*. Our Himmonda, the creator of our own Mahaverse in which this Universe has its place, is certainly not a Being of such nature.

The religions of this Earth are looked upon as ancient verities but in terms of the vastness of Time – even just the timespan of this planet Earth and its evolution – a few thousand years is but nothing; no time at all. However, whatever antiquity may be attributed to existing religious writings, they appear to have arisen from a primitive past. Whatever was the source of the wisdom expressed in those writings, that source did not it seems even know that the planet is not flat and that one could not fall off its edge into some fictional "abyss".

Our Himmonda – the creator of that section of the vast Cosmos in which revolves our own, relatively miniscule, planetary home – is not a creator of any "Hell" in which those who may not worship or believe in him will be banished to suffer eternal damnation; nor is our Himmonda the creator of any "Heaven" where the chosen are promised perpetual ecstacy. These are indeed primitive and, in terms of the fuller reality of the Laws of Life, simplistic and cruelly misleading concepts;

concepts which are therefore damaging to humanity for they are a deception to Truth. There are hellish and heavenly states. These are of our own creation. We certainly create our own dark or light conditions which are suffered or enjoyed within the physical and the stabilising dimensional worlds. And the Stabilising Self continues to experience its own earned state beyond death.

There is similar serious, insidious deception at work within the actions of prayer, worship and submission of the Will – which humankind has been instructed (nay commanded) to follow.

One cannot sow a pound of stupidity and reap a pound of knowledge or goodness. That is but simple logic. But that is what we expect to do. One understands the naivity of the searching human heart and mind and there does exist such a condition as *sincere* stupidity! Nonetheless, once recognised for what it is, it is surely folly to tolerate its continuance.

* * * *

In support of the exhortations of religion that we should submit our Will to God, it has been written: "*The Ocean becomes great by being* ***beneath*** *all the rivers*"... but the Truth which is TAYOZAAN asserts: "The Ocean becomes great by accepting all the rivers to itself". There is an enormous and profound difference between these statements: a difference in understanding, in the kind of action involved, in the direction in which one is moved and in the end result.

Man's Will, which he is exhorted to submit, is a most precious and indispensable facet and tool of his Life force. Our Will is the necessary requisite of any Self development. An increasingly refined action of Will is required in the science and art of Acceptance as it is taught in the philosophy of TAYOZAAN.

It must be reiterated that submission of our Will, to any force, can be highly dangerous; and it is a major example of wrong direction.

There are other such misconceptions, of subtle or blatantly wrong nature, which divert humanity from its correct spiritual direction.

Religions emphasise the need for *humility* but TAYOZAAN teaches *positive unity* – an incomparably more productive quality of Being to possess.

Fatalism, with which the psyche of millions is imbued, stems from a reliance on the influence of the stars (on planetary forces), on "God" or on some other kind of supernatural intervention: a passive stance of dependancy which bypasses or undermines our real need, which is for self effort.

A similar note of escape from responsibility lies in the concept that the physical world is but an illusion and that it should be abandoned. But it is just not possible to abandon the world. For the world is a reality *at its own dimensional level* and we are part of the reality of that dimension.

We cannot purchase peace by negating life. Peace is achieved when Life in its totality is mastered by an Acceptance involving all the dimensional depths; an Acceptance which knows that multi dimensional *Allness* as one's very Self. This inner stance and action of "Acceptance" is not of a superficial, flat nature. It has depthful and intelligent significance. The Acceptance taught within the philosophy of TAYOZAAN is an effective way of channelling the phenomenon of "experience" into the deeper dimension of the Seed of one's Existence; a purposeful action which feeds, refines and evolves the Light of Life within us. Prayer cannot bring us to that achievement.

Just as prayer will not put even a spoonful of rice in the mouths of the hungry, the same is true of inner hunger. Although spiritual food be available – in inexhaustible and magnificent supply – it requires us to first make the necessary effort to obtain and then agree, as it were, to actually "eat" it!

When mankind understands – and experiences – the correct route to growth and strength, he will continue to make his own efforts to nurture himself, and others, with food of both internal and external nature, knowing that no supernatural power will do this work for him.

Similarly, in the long, sad history of man's cruelty to man, no saving force has magically come to deliver the abused, no matter how pious he may be or how anguished and persistent be his prayer. The holocaust of Nazi Germany was but one of a myriad such examples. In that case it took the combined efforts of several nations to combat its evil. Force had to be employed against that dark force. Tangible effort has to be made by we ourselves to both provide for and protect ourselves. No God will do this for us.

On lighter note, and as a general, more mundane example, rather than to pray it is surely more fruitful to be honest, positive and helpful in our daily lives. To be of simple good cheer is a great help to others. Even a baby will respond happily to a smile. A smile brings sunshine into the day and, willy nilly, will affect all who see it. The person who shows helpful goodwill to others, even in quite simple ways, is of more help to life than a hundred praying souls.

* * * *

The Hindu religion speaks of the Kundalini Shakti, a "serpent" cosmic or occult power which lies sleeping at the base of the spine. The belief is that when awakened by yogic practices, this serpent power can eventually rise through and activate each of the seven main "Chakras" or nerve centres, five of which centres are situated at different points along the spinal column: the first being at the base of the spine, the second at the pelvic region and the third, fourth and fifth being respectively at the navel, heart and throat regions or centres. The last two Chakras, the sixth and seventh highest centres, are respectively that which is positioned between the eyebrows and that which is situated at the crown of the head. There are indeed such areas of internal dimensional significance.

The Hindu religion further teaches that one needs a wise Guru to take one through the process of awakening the Kundalini and that purity of being is first necessary otherwise the Kundalini power will not be able to ascend through the Chakras to reach its ultimate goal at the crown of the head.

The awakening of each such Chakra or centre is said to achieve for one extraordinary powers. One who awakens even the lowest Chakra is said to acquire full knowledge of the Kundalini, to acquire the ability to levitate and to have knowledge of the past, the present and the future, amongst other powers. The awakening of the second Chakra enables one, it is said, to have no fear of water, to have knowledge of astral entities; all one's negativities and impurities are destroyed and one conquers death. The third Chakra's awakening (that in the region of the navel) is said to gain one the power of acquiring hidden treasures and freedom from disease, leaving one free from the fear of fire. The conquerer of the Chakra at the heart centre is said to acquire (amongst other divine qualities) control over the element of air so that one can fly through the air and enter the body of another. The conquering through the Kundalini power of the Chakra at the throat centre it is said obtains imperishability and again, knowledge of the past, present and future. The awakening of the Chakra located at the region between the eyebrows enables one to become a freed soul whose karma of all past lives becomes destroyed; and on the Kundalini reaching the highest Chakra at the crown of the head, the yogi is said to be united with and to attain "God vision".

Many years ago I saw my own Kundalini. I have seen it stated in Hindu literature that the Kundalini actually has no form but that it is attributed a serpent's shape as the human mind needs some form to which it can relate – but in fact it has every appearance of a snake. The first occasion I saw it I had been sitting quietly, in reflective mood but certainly not with the Kundalini at all in mind (for I did not follow that philosophy or its yogic practices) when I experienced this spiritual snake at the crown of my head. I "saw" it with internal vision, for it belongs to the Stabilising dimension. And it spoke to my internal hearing. It said: "It has taken me twenty years to get here". I recognised the voice as my own. The Kundalini was indeed at the position of the highest Chakra but I certainly possessed no powers of levitation or the ability to fly nor would I consider myself to have attained "purity", to be free of my human negativities or to be possessed of the other divine attributes claimed to belong to the yogi with an awakened Kundalini which has arrived at the final Chakra at the crown of the head.

Nor have I ever encountered another mortal possessing the powers so claimed.

Some five years after my first experience of the Kundalini, having further progressed in the TAYOZAAN Systems and having further developed my ability to deal with Anti Life entities and forces, I recalled my experience of the Kundalini. I could not see what purpose it had of any positive nature. Moreover I did not like the idea of having this creature of the spirit world within my Being. I do not much care for snakes or, therefore, to be too close to them in the physical world so that I certainly did not relish having a spiritual one (in even closer proximity) internally! Moreover it had felt alien; not something to be cherished. I therefore decided I would apply myself to eradicating the Kundalini from my Being. As the thought occurred it instantly appeared within my internal vision. It was obviously fully aware of my intention and was in a great state of agitation. It raced up and down the area of my spinal column in swift, snakelike undulations as if trying to escape, but it could not. It was seemingly entrapped within my Being. I observed it for a few moments before transmuting its life into my Light: into the Seed of my Existence. I therefore no longer have my own personal Kundalini (or spiritual snake) existing within me.

The Hindu religion states that illumination comes only when the "Goddess" Kundalini awakens (this Goddess being said to be the source of all life) and that one should merge oneself in her. Again the exhortation is towards surrender of oneself to "God" – or, in this case to a "Goddess"; an exhortation to surrender oneself to this spiritual snake so allowing it to dominate one's internal being from a supreme vantage point. I could not (and do not) see that as at all correct. In fact absolutely to the contrary.

* * * *

Hinduism is full of mythological tales: stories which are stated as though truth but which are as fairy tales for children, as similarly are the tales in Greek mythology – although these are more adult in character. The stories are mainly improbable, impossible, or just sheer confusing nonsense: tales which need to be given some acceptable meaning through interpretation. Yet these tales hold much influence. The many characters within the stories, the numerous Gods, Goddesses or conceptualised Supreme Beings of the Hindu faith are still prayed to and worshipped to this day. It is a dream world of fantasy and unreality in which one goes round and round in circles, getting nowhere.

However, there are many truths to be experienced on our journey through this complex Existence which are as strange as some of those fictional products of the fertile human imagination.

As mentioned above, there does exist a "Kundalini" – or spiritual snake – of Anti Life nature, which belongs to an individual's Stabilising Self. There is also a Kundalini, or spiritual snake, of the World. This dark entity obstructs the portals to internal wisdom.

When searching internally – and coming close to penetrating the truth concerning the First Beginning of Creation – this dark serpent, the Kundalini of the World, suddenly disclosed itself. It reared itself before my internal vision, seemingly presenting me with a large, oblong egg which projected from each side of its mouth. It made sneakily swift, serpentine movements, which were as persuasive gestures to convince me that here, in its proferred egg, was the answer to my quest. I realised that it wished me to believe not only that this "egg" was the spiritual reality of the First Beginning of Creation but that the egg was its own; and, therefore, that it, the

Kundalini of the World, was the cause of the First Beginning of Creation. But I already knew the Kundalini of the human body (which had produced within me an instinctive aversion and distrust even on first encounter) to be of Anti Life nature. Therefore this external Kundalini, this dark spiritual serpent of the World, stood no chance of deceiving me. I recognised it was trying to distract me from further penetration into the Zero depths and from achieving the truth I sought. It was a clever attempt. But it failed.

* * * *

In fact it has been seen that we have *three* spiritual "snakes" of Anti Life nature operating within us. Such is the situation of each and every human being.

Of these three serpents one is of the Stabilising dimension of the Physical Worlds, the second is that which has its roots yet deeper within the Zero Worlds and the third is of the mysterious black counterpart of the Brimonda. Together they constitute the dark aspect of the nature of the *Life* which is the real Self of each of us; but fearsome (and perhaps horrifying) though this may strike us, we must not lose sight of the further understanding that when that innate imperfection has been totally transmuted, our Light, the Life which we are, will achieve its perfection.

The Kundalini of the Physical Worlds resides permanently within the human being but the other two Anti Life serpents can move and are free to come and go, at will. They are therefore able to enter and reside within us or leave us and operate in and from the outside World from time to time, as they please. But even if away from us they always retain a subtle connection for they belong to us. Of these two, one is the more powerful. It is the lowest and darkest force of a human being. It is that which belongs to the Black Brimonda.

These spiritual entities – which belong to and accompany each of us, both during life and after death - function at different depths or internal levels of our Being. They move intimately with us for they function within the Stabilising field of our human nervous system. These Kundalini forces therefore also accompany and move with the growth of the Light of our Life and continue to affect us even though we progress spiritually. For they too grow and gain strength as our Light matures; force always countering and counterbalancing force as the march of evolution continues.

As these spiritual Anti Life "snakes" function within the central nervous system, the spinal cord can still be said to be the region of their habitat within the physical body. Thought and feeling is therefore inescapably tainted by their influence. Although that influence be experienced by each individual at varying degrees of intensity and may only be in evidence from time to time, it is forever present, lurking just beneath the surface, for it is within the very fibres of our Being.

These forces cause us to suffer poor sleep with disturbed or nightmarish dreams. From time to time we will feel inexplicably drained of energy, for they sap our strength. In particular they affect and over stimulate the sexual energies and organs as they obtain power especially from this potent creative force.

The highest intelligence of our Mind and Light is therefore needed in order that we may be alive to -.and learn how to deal with - this oppressive condition, this living predicament of our Being. Whilst this "living predicament" simultaneously presents us with our living opportunity for spiritual maturity through the friction we meet in being subjected to their dark opposition, know that they are possessed of the advantage of having foreknowledge and that if we underestimate the subtlty, cunning and sheer power of those serpentine Anti Life forces, we do so at our peril.

The Kundalini – whether it be that which is within us or that which belongs to the World – is a poisonous force actively working against humankind. It is bent on obstructing our development and the achievement of our highest human destiny. It is its nature to be so.

The enemy is therefore closer than one may think.

* * * * *

The Kundalini snake has also been observed in another context. There was an occasion when I tried to see what has happened to those who have followed and served the God Krishna...and I observed a place within the spiritual Stabilising dimension where the devout – of all religious faiths – are resting. It was a swift but sharp view of what might be described as a spiritual resting ground for the prophets and leaders of various religious faiths and their followers. But although the place is akin to a cemetery, I saw that these Beings are not "dead". The Light of Life within each individual is still within their Stabilising form but their spirit "bodies" are prostrate and in deep sleep.

It is a vast place. These spirit forms lie in tomblike structures. There are rows upon rows of them stretching into the far distance in this grand "landscaped garden" of a world of incredible loveliness. The beauty of the place is in fact startling for it is full of flowers and glorious colours of pristine clarity; colours of remarkable perfection. In fact the whole place (this spiritual "world") impresses by its sheer perfection.

The "tombs" in this resting place of the Stabilising dimension are set amongst pathways, avenues and archways of blossom. It is apparent that some areas are occupied by those of a particular religious persuasion. One is aware that certain sections are Jewish, Christian, Islamic, Hindu and so forth, not only by visual impressions but by the atmosphere which is special to and of the nature of each faith. But it made no difference which faith a Being had belonged to; all were in the same state of deep sleep.

These various areas of religious faith were under canopies beautifully decorated with flowers, every blossom unchanging in its unblemished perfection, for the whole region is as it were frozen in time, completely still and soundless. Not a breath of wind disturbs nor is there light (nor, therefore, shade) nor is there warmth or cold.

It was apparent which were the resting places of the prophets and leaders of the various faiths, they being prominently esconced in edifices of prestigious grandeur whilst their close followers lay nearby and other devotees, in vast numbers, reposed in their individual tombs, stretching into the distance as far as the eye could see. Some tombs gave the appearance of being made of shining marble; others were crystalline. Therefore some spirit forms were visible where they lay; others were out of sight. But one knew they were there... and that they all slept.

The most prominent of the edifices was that occupied by Krishna. Krishna was seen to be in the form of the very

Kundalini snake with which his faith identifies. This spiritual serpent was reposing in a gold and silver dish or chalicelike receptacle on top of a tall column. This column was seen to be broad at its base and to narrow as it rises higher, the entire ornate structure being of great beauty for it is composed of precious stones of many hues. With the seeing was also the knowledge that this column supporting Krishna's resting place is the creative result of the stream of glorification projected towards this Being from his many followers on Earth. It was clear that the more Krishna is idolised and worshipped, the more this supporting column of precious gems grows – and the more entrapped he remains in his sleeping condition (as is the similar fate of other deified leaders – and their followers).

As I gazed, I saw Krishna's Kundalini form try to awaken itself. This was the only movement I observed in that place of rest. His serpentine body endeavoured to raise up. Twice it tried whilst I viewed him but each time he slumped back, unable to overcome the power of sleep which holds all who are there. I tried, with the sincere willing of my Mind, to help him awaken and felt compassion for all those pious, dedicated souls who languish in that frozen state of beauty; but so far as I know, they all sleep on.

Whether these sleeping souls dream whilst in their entombed state of spiritual sleep, I know not; but beautiful though it be, that spiritual mausoleum is not an end I would ever wish for myself. Nor would I wish any Being whom I love to be condemned to such an end by my prayers and adulation. It is no wonder that our Himmonda was so severe in his injunction that we should not worship him or beg him in prayer but that we should work towards the development of the Light of Life within our own Beings. For, unwitting though we may be as to the end result of our devotions and sincerely dedicated though we may be, the action of worship and prayer is seen to imprison both ourselves and the Beings to whom we project our thoughts and emotions.

No matter what trauma may have occurred to the physical body, the Stabilising body is seen to remain whole and unaffected after our physical demise, with the individual's Light still housed within the Mind of its Stabilising Self. Upon death our Light and its Stabilising Self are naturally freed from the physical body. And *if it be sufficiently developed,* our Light is also freed from its Stabilising form. It is therefore clear that the ancient practice of bursting the physical skull following death in the belief that this is needed in order to free the spiritual content of a Being from its physical form, is totally unnecessary and is of nil effect.

* * * *

Even a slight disorientation in understanding can eventually lead to major deflection from the right route. This has happened with the doctrines of desirelessness and renunciation. As we can see, where such an attitude of mind has become endemic through years of belief in non-attachment and treating the world as illusory and unimportant, there has been little advance in human progress. The standard of living is very poor. Movement is slow.

Detachment does not equate with a state of connected control. Add desirelessness to non attachment and one has mixed a lethal cocktail which can only spell disaster in this physical world.

Where these two attitudes co-exist en masse – especially when justified by religious teaching and glorified by sincerity of heart – the very core of a society as affected. It becomes part of the fabric of the society's culture, influencing all activity even if only weakly adhered to. Should the exhortations and expectations of religion towards detachment and desirelessness be truly employed, the nation concerned would crumble. And should the world follow suit and we all follow the doctrine of detachment and desirelessness, one can easily predict the result. Life on Earth would collapse.

The more fully we are positively connected to Life the more we can gain control. Whether we like it or not, we have to be attached to this living process to survive. And desire is also fundamental to the process of survival. Moreover desire, *when properly motivated and directed*, is a force necessary to the attainment of perfection. For it is also our desire – of a more refined nature – which impells us to higher achievement. In fact, as we progress, we see that the force of desire never leaves us but that, in common with our other attributes of Will and Intelligence, it merely changes in its depth of quality. A Zero Being therefore becomes *by nature* desireless of that which is gross. But the desire of a Being who achieves Zero dimensional level becomes increasingly altruistic and more magnanimously expansive.

* * * *

We should not go against the flow of the evolutionary river but we need to move, intelligently and gratefully, faster than the ordinary flow to speed up the evolutionary process of Creation. Our aim is to consciously accellerate the maturing movement of Life itself.

This totally different approach produces an attitude of grateful appreciation towards the World. Those who foster non attachment and view the World as illusory and therefore of no value, fear desire. They develop an attitude which is akin to non appreciation. If given something, or if they are not, they try to feel equally unmoved. They effect to show neither pleasure nor appreciation and the words "Please" and "Thank you" are not common to the vocabulary of those whose culture has developed the stance of "non attachment and desirelessness within a world which is illusory". It is not surprising that this leads to an outlook of dull disinterest. Poor standards in habitat and personality are the inevitable result.

As it is in the nature of things that instruction from deeper understanding eventually degenerates into a distorted form, it is so very important to question teachings, to question one's own understanding and to see what is the actual fruit of one's beliefs and actions.

* * * *

Many so called "spiritual" activities can be clearly seen by those exercising but ordinary common sense, to be sadly misguided or actually wrong – wrong in fact to the point of sickness.

There are many cults and religions where adherents work themselves into states of trance and are actually taken over by Anti Life demonic forces. Although they open themselves to dark possession, this is considered desirable "spiritual" experience and they will return to their meeting places, time after time (with relish moreover) to repeat this highly dangerous practice. There are those who worship rats, who believe they will receive blessing by eating the food offerings placed for the rats, contaminated though the food be by the rodents' urine and droppings. Then there are the Sadhus who behave in bizarre ways to prove their spirituality, standing perhaps on one leg for long periods of time or abusing their bodies in many other ways; abuse stemming from pathetic ignorance for this is maltreatment of their precious physical vehicle which should instead be cared for with respect and gratitude and be employed in positive action. But these Sadhus take vows which defy the logic of normality, submitting themselves to various forms of self inflicted torture of mind, emotion and body, giving nothing to the world but on the contrary depending on the labours of others for food. Nor can they achieve anything but minimal gain for themselves (apart from strengthening their powers of endurance), such self brutilising way of life and endeavour being unhealthfully imbalanced.

The Aghoris of India live (if "live" be the appropriate word) amongst the dead at cremation grounds and have such a concept of reality that they will consume the flesh of human corpses from funeral pyres. As I understand it, these Aghoris align themselves with the dark aspect of creation, believing they need to "be" that dark aspect. But such an endeavour towards spirituality is surely an engagement in depravity: abysmal depavity. This is a clear example of how the reasoning of mankind can deceive itself and justify behaviours which are totally unacceptable when seen from saner viewpoint. One can be aware of a partial aspect of reality and behave towards it in a totally unhealthful, unbalanced way. It is incredible that such an indignity to the human dead could be tolerated by any nation in this day and age. It is also hard to imagine a mental state which would wish to consume rotting corpses, death no doubt having come from old age and/or disease. This is surely an example of civilisation crawling on its belly; a condition of degeneration far, far removed from true spirituality.

Yet Sadhus are generally venerated in their homelands and enjoy "holy" status. Their conduct is in general much respected. They may even earn the status of

Sainthood. Their dedication may indeed be strong but how sad it is to waste such dedication in fanatically wrong or useless directions. In some instances they may reap a degree of positive return for their pains but mostly the fruits of such ways of life can only be poor or, as in the case of the Aghoris, horrendously dark.

One would have expected the powerful religions which have exerted such strong influence on Earth over these past thousands of years, to have long since secured the establishment of the basic humanities: the simple basic virtues of kindness, respect and decent conduct. But one can clearly see that such basic quality of life on Earth has not been achieved. Moreover, as history confirms, religions divide. Untold cruelties, torture and millions of violent deaths have been perpetrated over the centuries by and in the name of religion, fuelled by that insatiable thirst for power and domination which bedevils the human psyche. And, extraordinarily, we do not – or perhaps in fairness it is more correct to say that we *cannot* – learn from the past sufficiently well to empower change. Nothing of the dark side of our nature changes, except in the style and degree of sophistication of our bad behaviour. Many parts of the world still remain in the barbaric past. It is as though an endemic insanity lurks within human nature. And that madness continues to erupt. We seem powerless to control it. So-called "ethnic cleansing" is not new to our experience. It has been occurring here and there from time to time throughout the centuries. Human beings – or one might more accurately say beings who have the appearance of being human – assume fiendlike content and will rape, mutilate and murder, become possessed of an energy of rampant destruction, goaded on by such feelings of hatred and rejection that they want to eliminate others from the very face of the Earth. No amount of prayer will help the afflicted. No heavenly hand comes to open the gates of the torture chamber or the concentration camp to free the oppressed or to stay the upraised hand of the tormentor. Although religions tell tales of past miracles and base their faith on divine assistance, it just does not occur. Adherants conveniently turn a blind eye to this anomoly. Where is that all merciful God – whom we are told intervened in various extraordinary ways in times past – on the many occasions (beyond count) since then of similar, or even greater, pitifully abject human need?

The qualities of mercy and compassion, of loving magnanimity of heart and mind, are assuredly not strained on this Earth. There are such obvious and continuing injustices, humanity towards humanity. How is it possible for the caste system of India still to be tolerated? How can it be that those of so-called "high" caste have not long since totally rejected such an injustice? Despite the privilege and benefit of education and travel, the ruling classes do not appear to have come to see it as shameful to regard other human beings as "untouchable". They do not seem to see their attitude of arrogant superiority and the ongoing disadvantagement of others to be just that: arrogant superiority and privilege at the expense of the disadvantaged. To the nation's shame, a system is maintained which condemns vast numbers of its people to lives of poverty and little respect whilst the privileged continue to enjoy the riches of high position. Such inhumanity is still, even to this present time, justified by many on religious grounds although, when seen with the clear eye of justice, it is actually a form of racism within the race: a form of discrimination which has been so cemented within the psychology of a nation over such long passage of time that its acceptance as "normality" is hard to break.

Until quite recent times India, a civilisation in being for over five thousand years, has also allowed the ancient practice of Suttee (or Sati) to continue. The country's "holy" men, on whose guidance the populace habitually placed their faith, maintained Suttee – that is the suicide of a widow by throwing herself upon her husband's funeral pyre and being burned alive with his corpse – to be a noble act; something expected of her by society, her duty and therefore her inescapable fate. The mere idea is horrific and repugnant to the emancipated and I applaud with all my heart the sanity and courage of that nation which put an end, by law, to such a practice.

It is of no real surprise that the practice of Suttee was the brainchild of the male of the species. Nor, therefore, is it of any suprise that there was no reuirement for the husband to suffer similar fate and commit Suttee should his wife predecease him. It does not appear that anyone dared give voice to this blatant inequality. It is extraordinary that even today, some Hindu Pandits or Swamis still justify the practice of Suttee, considering it to be a noble act; and they will state, with utmost conviction, that the caste system was the greatest social system ever devised for mankind. They imply, moreover, that if one does not see it as such, then one just does not enjoy their depth of understanding.

The male of the species, the physically stronger gender, has managed his environment for his own advantage, with his own self interests in mind. Religion is a means of justification for many restrictive practices although in reality it has been man himself who has brought such practices into being in order to maintain control, to ensure that women and the populace at large remain held firmly in subjugation.

It is the male phallus, the "lingam" which has been made an object worship and remains a religious symbol for millions to this day.

Although the feminine aspect of creativity is also venerated, the female force, symbolised by the female sexual organ – the "yoni" of Hindu faith – is far less in evidence as a subject of worship than is the male phallus whose shape is incorporated in the domes and minarets of religious architecture throughout the globe, from East to West. Whilst religions acknowledge the combined male and female element within creation, the ascendant, predominantly motivating and more powerful force is generally accepted to be that of masculine nature; of which viewpoint the male of the human specie has taken full advantage.

It is the female, not men, who must shroud themselves in clothing, to the extent of even covering the face and hair from view, harsh punishment being meted to offenders in some countries if this ruling is not strictly adhered to. Such requirement is tantamount to an admission that men, despite their religious endeavours, remain so weak and ignoble of being that they cannot behold merely the face or hair of a woman without being tempted to lust after her. Why do they not themselves suffer this unnatural restraint and inconvenience by covering their own bodies in this way? Why do they not cover their own heads and faces against similar temptation from the opposite sex, or is this an admission that women are by nature more disciplined, that they are possessed of a more innate nobility of being than the male and that there is no need to fear lowly response from the female's beholding of the human form?

The woman has long been held responsible for the alleged "original sin" and spiritual fall of mankind. She has suffered a legacy of guilt from the alleged weakness of one woman in the long distant past: that of the mythological Eve in her succumbing to temptation in the Garden of Eden. Moreover – also with strong religious backing – womankind has suffered the further injustice and stigma of having her bodily procreative functions deemed "unclean". As the male actively participates in human procreation and his own bodily functions are very much involved, one would not have expected such blatant prejudice, such sheer *hypocrisy*, could have survived; but it has.

However, female subjection by the male (as is evident to the present time) has been so constant over the centuries that, ironically, women have themselves to a large extent accepted and even perpetuated their own oppressed condition. The covering up of the female form to such an extreme degree has assumed a nun-like preciousness and it is therefore a cause of actual distress to many women should society suggest the practice be abolished. However, many women are now of different view and they do see through many such requirements and attitudes as a perpetuation of the historic reality of male domination – a domination born and maintained out of male self interest. Many women now demand change but in too many parts of the world males still maintain supremacy, keeping women at their bidding and economically imprisoned for their entire existence. Too many women continue to bear the brunt of the workload, are kept in positions of low status and little respect, helplessly subjected to many injustices and indignities. This state of affairs has largely been imposed and justified by the edicts of religion: in other words by the inventions and imposed authority of the dominant male of the human specie.

* * * *

We are strangely locked into negative postures of thought, attitude and behaviour which strangle and make mockery of justice yet we passively accept that it continues thus until someone or some emancipated body of people have the clarity, courage and resolve to speak out and try to effect change.

Religious Nazism does not just exist as part of the historical memory of our barbarous past. It is still, to the shame of those guilty ones who perpetuate it, with us to this day. To mutilate another, to amputate limbs by way of punishment for crime, to stone to death, to issue or carry out a Death "Fatwa" (a Death Sentence) on someone for not honouring or for speaking against another's religious beliefs – or even, as is the practice in some Islamic countries, for merely leaving the Muslim faith – is truly a crime in itself. It is savagely immoral, a response totally devoid of spiritual quality. And to attempt to justify such Fatwas or edicts of judgment as being commands of the religion concerned is, additionally, an indictment against the religion itself. For that which is of Truth does not need to obliterate anything that opposes it. That which is of high level knows all Life as of itself in the Oneness of Reality. It is itself all that is and all that is not. Truth stands invincible. Nothing can harm it. Nothing can detract from it.

Man either is of the Truth or he is not. Whatever his views, whatever be his response to another's views, Truth remains untouched. Therefore any person who denies or speaks ill of the Himmonda can do so without fear of having a Death "Fatwa" or any other harming judgmental edict issued against them by anyone who gives their loyalty or allegience to the truths expressed in the philosophy of TAYOZAAN. The Himmonda cannot be harmed. He is what He is: THE INVISIBLE, INVINCIBLE, NON-EXISTENT, LOVING, GRATEFUL, COMPASSIONATE LIGHT. He is inviolable. It is only they who deny Truth, who are the losers. Everyone is free to think or say what they may. Anyone is free to criticise, or even ridicule or revile TAYOZAAN and/or the Himmonda, the Creator of this our Mahaverse. The Law of Life, however, remains and will be the inexorable arbiter.

It must here be said that, despite there being so much evident misunderstanding within the Hindu religion as it manifests today, some of which misunderstanding has been criticised in this chapter, TAYOZAAN is the projected depth of Aryan Hinduism in action; for from that Eastern source of knowledge came the truths which are termed "Brahman", the Unity or Oneness of Life, and the evolutionary process of Reincarnation – ***for which I am eternally grateful***.

QUALITIES AND SPIRITUAL ALCHEMY

What are we without qualities? Qualities are all that distinguish us from being mere robots. Quality of Being is the only truly substantive difference between human beings which is of any real importance.

Without values we are without direction, bobbing aimlessly like corks on the tidal waves of Time's perpetual motion, subject to life's every whim. So strong is Time's tide...forever agitating us over the superficial crust of our existence. Without the constraint of discipline, without the motivation of values which can give us some measure of self orientation, we find ourselves precipitated forward on that tide of life's inexorable movement to where we may not choose to be. Conversely, we may find ourselves gripped by the powerful suction of life's ebbing tides so that not only are we not able to go forward to positively free ourselves from unsatisfactory circumstances but we feel actually opposed, pushed backwards, our lives somehow caught in a downward spiral of negative force. Or there are times when we just feel as it were becalmed, vacuous, lacking motivation, lacking opportunity for change.

Most of us are securely locked within this imprisoned situation by reason of our existent condition of Being. We are actually imprisoned by and within *what we are*. In all honesty we have eventually to acknowledge that our failures and disappointments lie not so much in the outer circumstances of our lives but in the fault of our own responses to those circumstances.

The answer to acquiring at least some degree of liberation from the bondage of cause and effect, the way towards greater freedom in enjoyment of enhanced self-motivation in the expression of one's true Self, lies in the strength of our qualities. And we see that the route forward, the means of achieving such emancipation, lies in the exercise of intelligent control.

As this Book of TAYOZAAN has endeavoured to convey, by means of intelligent awareness and right action we can produce a qualitied *substance* of Being which is freer by its very nature. With rightly directed effort, we can gradually produce a "wholesome" and therefore stronger inner identity of Being of quality, the natural outcome of which is also the obtaining of self respect. We all need to have a healthful sense of our own worth, not to harbour destructive feelings of self-contempt for our own lacks and weaknesses. In fact above all we need to be at peace with and respect ourselves. We need to establish within ourselves the comfort of a qualitied identity of selfhood which not only those near to us (whose acceptance we cherish) can value and respect but which we ourselves can view with clear conscience, find acceptable and, with quiet dignity, value.

* * * *

The Mind, that "thinking jewel" which is our organ of expression and the instrument via which we can create a Self of Light of the eternal nature, is known by its qualities. Mind also reflects the qualities of the deeper Self of our Light. When a higher state of Mind and Light is achieved we are possesssed of a composite of qualities which can be summarised as **Love, Joy, Intelligence, Knowledge, Wisdom, Gratitude, Strength, Compassion**.

Every facet of the spectrum of this composite of qualities is at varying depth and level of refinedness and strength within each of us. Each facet has to be further nourished and honed. Such internal growth takes a lifetime of ever intensifying, subtle effort. It is not easily come by. Development of this nature has, therefore, to be earned but when achieved, such growth – the ever deepening maturity of these noble human qualities – belongs both to one's Self of the Unutterable or Non Existent dimensional Light (to whatever level one's Seed of Existence may have reached) and to its functioning organ: the Mind; "Mind", as has previously been clarified, being distinct from "brain" (the brain being the physical tool of our Mind).

Our Mind and Light are conjoined, so close is the two-way flow of energy and expression – from Light to Mind and from Mind to Light. As development of Mind into the depths of our Light progresses, our qualities mature into the Zero dimensions and are subtly empowered. With maturity into the Zero depths our qualities are energised; strengthened. This strength of the nature of Zeroness is a force...a power.

Intentional endeavour to attain quality of Mind in pursuit of higher level of Selfhood requires the employment of at least the first glimmerings of the very qualities sought to be achieved. Evolution, in its relatively mechanical process does, perforce, eventually produce increased sensitivities and qualities. So that by the time one comes to make choice to *consciously* co-operate with the process, the Being has already been "honed" to have a measure of intelligence and to have developed other qualities to varying degrees of intensity; but I think we would all concede, if we are honest with ourselves, that our emotional and mental content is by no means as perfect or mature as it might be or as we would wish it to be. Doubtless most of us would agree we have need to acquire and live by infinitely higher qualities of Being than we at present possess or employ.

* * * *

We need Intelligence to be able to evaluate, combined with the passion of Sincerity. We need to see what lacks in the very qualities which we do perhaps already (at least to some degree) possess.

Even if we have a sympathetic nature, Sympathy without Wisdom can be merely a vacuous support for weakness and therefore of little use to life, producing nothing more than a placebo effect – or worse, for sympathy devoid of wisdom can actually encourage ignoble weakness in another. Similarly Empathy, without clearminded Objectivity, can cause one to be drawn into and become lost in another's negative condition of being. In that case there is no gain to either party.

Strength devoid of Sensitivity can degenerate into hardness. Strength must not be like granite. Strength needs to be complemented by Understanding, by Wisdom and Compassion to be of truly helpful, noble quality.

In the same way Dispassion and Objectivity, excellent though these qualities may be, can cause a person to be remote and coldly aloof. At its extremity, dispassionate objectivity shows neither compassion, regret nor remorse if "heart", if Love, be lacking.

Control and Discipline can be negatively rigid, a pain to oneself and to others, if it is not accompanied by a breadth of Vision, if there be no reasonable Flexibility or Tolerance to moderate it.

Patience needs Wisdom to know when it should be applied. There are times for forwarding action, not restraint. Wisdom itself contains Patience inherently within it.

Simplicity without intelligent depth and magnanimity of spirit is a quality standing on emptiness and weakness. But Simplicity expressed from the depth of high quality of Being is nobility personified. Conversely, Magnanimity without the discipline of wise restraint or moderation can go overboard. Magnanimity needs the balancing grace of Simplicity to give it ennobling quality.

Consciousness, or Awareness – so important though it be – standing alone can be merely what may be described as an "active passivity" for it goes nowhere without further functioning action. Creativity, movement from the deep intelligence, is additionally required for that consciousness to be activated so that growth takes place. So many meditational practices bring one merely to this point of "active passivity" and no further.

Therefore each "good" quality can be flawed if there be a lack of other, sufficiently strong, compensating and constructive qualities to balance it. One good quality standing alone without other necessary enhancing qualities can cause us to function unproductively or to create blatant negativity. We clearly need to acquire and behave from a balanced blend of qualities.

* * * *

The quality of Love may be inspired in us by another, but that Love is one's own. It may appear to be the particular object of such Love who is responsible for the emotion but that Love belongs to the depth of being of he or she who loves. The inspiration for Love's arising may be removed but the capacity for and ability to love is the treasure of the Being who has loved. That treasure remains his or her own content which cannot be removed. It cannot be taken away. The capacity for Love can be covered over by hurt, by grief, but it cannot be extracted from us. Once earned our quality of Being continues with us from this existence into our next incarnation.

The same truth applies to other sensitivities. The beauty one sees is, quite truly "in the eye of the beholder". A flower is a flower but it is the viewer whose quality of being beholds its beauty. It is the viewer who is able to make connection with the beholden object and who responds from his or her own quality of love, of gratitude and appreciative sensitivity. There are many who have no "eye" for beauty, little sensitivity to quicken their quality of Loving Gratitude.

"Justice" is not some arbitrary set of rules for man to follow in order to maintain social order but it is that which represents a moral depth of total fairness. To be truly Just is not easy. Justice equates with maturity. It is a superb quality. It is, like Love, Gratitude, Wisdom and Compassion, one of the great qualities one would expect to be possessed by Supreme Beings.

The whole quality of our existence depends very much on what we are, for our content affects how each of us relates to our every experience of living. We each of us have our own individual viewpoints and therefore our own individual responses towards every experience which enters our awareness. The point of view and the response can vary enormously from person to person. Very much depends on the level of the individual's Being and the qualities functioning at point of reception of experience as to what response may eventuate.

* * * *

The attainment of qualities goes hand in hand with the achievement of higher dimensional levels of Being. Like the Alchemist, we need to transform the base material which we are. We also need to transform the material which continues newly to enter our experience during our many lives lived in this gross manifest world.

The practical Systems of TAYOZAAN achieve this transforming process. The aim is to transform and eventually to truly transmute all that which – as Beings of both finite and infinite nature and therefore of multi-dimensional experience – constitutes our living "reality" within this manifest world. This transformation, this eventual gradual *transmutation* of the living material of our Life as it is lived, produces a subtle refinedness of our very essence into quality of Zero dimensional nature, until we eventually become pure spiritual Gold: a Life whose substance is of the eternal nature of enduring Timeless quality and is, therefore, of immeasurable value.

The age-old dream of man being able to turn base metal into gold is no fable in internal terms provided appropriate action is taken to move the inner content to positive change. Such internal movement is taught within the philosophy of TAYOZAAN, the basic cornerstone of whose teaching is acceptance of experience to our Seed of Existence *with qualities*. This action truly effects change. The requisite tools for this kind of creative action are the refined Intelligence, Will and sincerity of Desire. The greater the depth of Zeroness involved in this process the more subtly potent is the act, until the action truly becomes one of actual transmutation.

* * * *

When possessed of even a modicum of the higher qualities of Being one is just not able to wantonly cause hurt or harm to any other living creature or to despoil anything. Moreover, with increasing wisdom, one is more easily able to discriminate and distinguish that which is alien to those higher qualities. One is gradually better able to recognise the adulteration and impurities which emanate from Life's Anti Life negativity in all its devious, manipulative and deceptive forms.

With increasing wisdom, there therefore comes greater clarity in discerning that which requires further transformation within our own Being. It also, of course, makes one more sensitive to all that is gross in the world outside of us; but when we have achieved enough knowledge, experience and strength we will be better able to bring the appropriate qualitied responses into action in both our inner and our outer lives.

ALL LOVE, GRATITUDE AND COMPASSION BE OUR LIGHT. GREAT PURPOSE, CLARITY, INTELLIGENCE, KNOWLEDGE AND WISDOM, COURAGE AND STRENGTH BE OUR LIGHT. **GLORY BE THE LIGHT OF *ALL* LIFE**.

* * * *

Man's limited concept of this our planetary home, viewed from our antlike position upon the Earth's crust within the geographic confines of the country in which we live our daily lives, bears no comparison to the reality of our position which is beheld when Earth is viewed from an orbiting Satellite. From such a vantage point there is a gloriously expansive, vastly more holistic view of our planet. The artificial divisions of countries, nationalities and race melt away. National borders are invisible. Only land masses set in vast areas of ocean are apparent. For one who enjoys such an experience, his former concept of Earth – with its manmade demarcations and set boundaries over which nations have fought with vicious zeal for millenia – must surely evaporate. He must surely then see mankind's customary notion of his place on Earth as some cruel and nonsensical illusion. For millenia large groups of people have deluded themselves that they have right of ownership to the patch of the planet on which they have been born – land which, in greed and ignorance, they have coveted with vicious inhumanity, segregating themselves moreover by unnatural racial and religious divisions. It is an illusion long suffered as in an unending bad dream; a bad dream which, sadly, continues.

To observe the Earth revolving in space – together with, but dwarfed into relative insignificance by the vast cosmos of stars surrounding us on all sides out into the black depths of infinite space – makes irrelevant the idea of North, South, East or West, or what is "up" or what is "down". If we could all actually experience the physical reality of this whole Earthly planet spinning its own path within the cosmos in the vastness of its own timescale, we could surely never be quite the same again. At very least it should be a salutary lesson which should shock us into realising the stupidity of the usually smallminded and blinkered condition in which life is lived on this planet.

Similarly, when beginning to become possessed of the quality of higher dimensional Being, one becomes privy to a vastly different perspective. One's view of Life assumes a breadth, a depth, a subtlty and magnanimity of vision quite beyond that previously held, opening up an entirely new comprehension concerning our existence.

* * * *

Inherent in wisdom is eternal patience, that condition of deeper intelligent control which lies in the creative zone beyond ordinary reason. That "zone" is a place within; a place within our own globule of inner space. And the totality of qualities which is represented by the word "TAYOZAAN" is an active, living state – of differing dimensional depths – belonging to the Light or Seed of Existence within that internal zone.

As we progress we are able to live far more "alivedly". When we are more "alive" there is then possibility of functioning more constructively in the present moment. To be "alive" brings sense of fulfilment. Otherwise we are only semi awake. We respond mechanically from our old content of past experience. We become lost in daydreams. We are as if magnetised by the outer world's impingement upon our senses, our attention being propelled outward – and forward in time. We are forever straining blindly into the future, rushing into the next moment, never being fully alive in and to the present moment. But our Tomorrow is actually in Today, for what we are today predestines our Tomorrow. Our Yesterday is also within Today, for all our Yesterdays are what we now are. Therefore Today, the present moment, is the "Rolling Present" for this moment contains within it Past, Present *and Future*. It is invaluable to have sense of this truth as we then appreciate for ourselves the importance of the present moment, in understanding that our Future is truly dependant upon how we are in our Today.

As we progress we endeavour to *Be*, not just in this present moment of existential Time, but in the Eternal Moment within Time. When functioning in the Eternal Momentedness, we *stop*. We are then poised within the internal space of a totally different dimensional nature. We taste, we are connected with, Timelessness – whilst yet still fully aware of and acting in the finite dimensional reality. That Timeless Eternal Present is within each moment of Time; and finite Time: past, present and future, is held within that Eternal Moment.

When in touch with the eternal reality there is neither need nor urge to continue to rush like the proverbial demented Lemming en route to its own destruction. We then know we have arrived where we truly belong. We are at home within ourselves. Nothing lures us for we are fulfilled and there is glorious, all-pervading peace. But one can never in this existence rest on one's laurels. Always it is necessary to remain attentive, to make effort to remain truly "alive" and in control, ever sensitive to maintain the quality of Being which gives us entre to and enables us to stay within that eternal qualitied place, for without such vigilence and right effort it is only too easy to slip back into an unawakened, grosser dimensional level of existence.

Once there is a taste of that eternal Timeless position of freedom, the truth of our usual condition of enslavement and ignorance will be realised and it will be understood how abnormal – how truly horrible – is our usual unawakened state. The difference, the contrast in state is vast; quite literally worlds apart.

It is, however, a strange but true fact of Life's multi-dimensional reality that as soon as we are reduced to awareness only of the gross dimensional level of physical Existence, that illuminating insight, that realisation which we had enjoyed, is lost to us – even forgotten. If remembered, it is but as a distant memory for the experience was that belonging to a different world. It belonged to a higher dimensional strata of our experiencing. When we slump back within our grosser level of Being, that unaware, beclouded part of us has little or no affinity with such internal sunlight. We again become oblivious as to our condition. We slot back into the old groove. Our Light is hidden, the Mind sits back apathetically and lets life flow over it, influence it and dominate it again. The true Self and higher Mind are no longer in the driving seat. We return to square one.

Is it not true, loth though we may be to admit it, that we normally have little real choice but to go whither the winds of life blow us? Our awareness is magnetised outwards by the demands on our attention of the material world. The world holds our senses enthralled. We are pulled this way and that like puppets. We are at the mercy of the hands of a capricious puppeteer. We easily become "lost" in our experiences; "lost" in the very often quite mechanical activity of our brain which is allowed to go on its own merry – or not so merry – way like some out of control machine. We function like a computer whose electric current is running amok producing images, conversations and sometimes quite bizarre imagined situations which stimulate a plethora of emotion – much of which is tainted with negativity; for the things which are particularly "on our mind" and which trouble us: our fears, resentments and rejections, come forward the most readily, as also do our more disturbing and agitating desires and strivings. It is therefore we ourselves, our own brains, which manufacture and are responsible for much of the discontent and lack of peace which we suffer.

How to transform this sad condition of being is surely the most valuable of all educations; precious, lifegiving knowledge to be eagerly sought. The possibility of transmutation of the base material which we are into the Timeless freedom of Eternal Being is surely treasure trove beyond all earthly wealth.

* * * *

As has already been explained, the internal Light is a living force differing in its brilliance and depths of quality from person to person and from time to time within the same person according to the point of development each individual may have reached at any given stage of their evolution (subject also to his or her fluctuations in state as life is lived, for no one state can be constantly maintained). That Light is visible to the internal eye.

One of the Aphorisms in Part Two of this book states that the symbol of the Star of David is one of the highest known to man. I know it as a symbol of that Light... of that Love... of the Eternal dimensions. The statement and the knowledge result from two specific viewings or experiences which occurred on separate occasions, years apart one from the other.

There is a point, or spot, at the centre of the forehead from which radiates the Unutterable Light (or the yet deeper internal Light if one has achieved such further depth of Being). In one of the experiences to which I refer I saw such a Light radiating from my own brow. It formed a triangular downwards irradiation, the apex of the triangle being at the centre of the brow. On the other occasion of which I speak, the apex of the triangle was again at the middle of the forehead but this time the irradiation rayed in an upwards "V" of Light.

The Light of the downwards triangle rests on the quality of Gratitude. The Light of the upwards triangle is seated on the quality of Compassion. Both triangles of Light carry the quality of Love but the upwards triangle which stands on Compassion carries the most intense quality of Love. The colour of the Light at the apex of the upwards "V" was of a reddish orange hue but as my gaze travelled upwards its colour changed into ever lightening shades of yellow until the light yellow assumed a transparency. The higher my vision travelled upwards into the widening triangular ray of Light the more intense was the experience of Love. At that stage of my development the intensity so vibrated my being that eventually I could bear the experience no longer. No longer could I hold my gaze towards that transparent luminosity. I could neither stand the increasing intensity of Light nor bear the intensity of the vibration of such a quality of Love with which it was increasingly vivified. I could therefore look no more.

The two directions of the triangles – the downward and the upward "V"s of Light – were not closed along their bases but were open ended. The Light rayed out from the centre of the brow in both directions with no visible end to the emanation When the two triangles of emanation are brought together, there one has the symbol known on Earth as the Star of David. It surely depicts an eternal Truth. That living state of Eternity can be neither emptied, filled nor stopped.

The emanations of Gratitude and Compassion from each triangular irradiation of Light are powerful forces. The downwards emanation, the force of Gratitude, of Loving Gratitude, is the quality of creativity: the force of blessing which, when arising from the Zero dimensional depths with sufficient intensity of eternal quality, is an act of cosmic procreation.

It was an internal act of acceptance of our Universe – actually an acceptance of the wisdom and destiny of our Universe – to the Seed of my Existence, imbued with an intensity of quality of Loving Gratitude, which produced for me firstly an internal viewing of that great cosmic creature, our Universe. Subsequent to that experience, as a result of ever more expansive and depthful acts of acceptance in state of love and intense gratitude, there followed the further viewings of our vast Brimonda which I have already described in the foregoing chapters concerning the Cosmology of TAYOZAAN.

In such an act of acceptance (as "acceptance" is understood and practiced in TAYOZAAN) the cosmos stays where it is but it is the Zero dimensional reality of that which is being accepted which is taken into the depths of one's Seed of Existence. It is a definite and purposeful act. The quality of Loving Gratitude within the act produces Oneness. Oneness is the internal connection, the avenue of accomplishment which opens one to the possibilities which are within the nature of the Zero dimensions. The greater be the depth of one's Zeroness of Being, the more evolved one is; and the greater become one's possibilities of achievement within the Zero Worlds. This is the route to Perfection.

* * * *

In the same Aphorism as that in which I speak of the Star of David, I refer to the Nazi Swastika as being the symbol of darkness, the symbol of the Anti Life forces or the "Black Brahman".

This Nazi symbol of the swastika represents the dark aspect of creation. It represents the lowest, grossest life force; a force which at its own grossest end is utter evil. There is no insect, animal or other living form produced by nature (however predatory and vicious) as low as that dark force which is represented by the Nazi Swastika; but that evil influence assuredly does exist. It manifests through living forms.

That dark force, the Anti Life aspect of creation, has been seen in the form of a spinning black cross. The ancient artists' impression of such a spinning movement could well account for the bent arms of the cross in the Nazi form of the Swastika, thus indicating in graphic form the direction of the movement of crossed bars. However, knowing the field of its nature and influence this is never a symbol to be exalted by man, representing as it does a force of baser order than the dust under one's feet. On the contrary, the force this symbol represents needs to be understood for what it is, controlled and finally irradicated. This is a very necessary aspect of spiritual achievement in the march towards the transformation and eventual transmutation of our Being. However, as previously clarified, the dark aspect of Life does have its very definite purpose and when I viewed that black spinning cross the message it conveyed within its spinning was a "smiling" reassurance that *I should not worry....* but it has taken me many years to understand that message and to work on the mastering of the Anti Life reality, the Black Brahman, for its opposition is to be found at every dimensional level.

* * * *

Our Unutterable Self, which is of the creative dimensional nature, is capable of achieving Brahman level of creativity at the height of its maturity, but even he who reaches Brahman level requires yet further transmutation, for the creative state is still one of bondage. The achievement of Brahman level is not total fulfilment of our destiny. It is not, by far, the end of the road.

The Unutterable Dimension of creativity is also the creator of Anti Life and is therefore also the source of life's disharmony. The creational field is not "wicked" but its nature is causation and effect. The Unutterable dimension is the activating forcefield behind and within physical manifestation. It is also the forcefield which inspires Life towards the higher internal dimensions. It constantly activates. Its creativity has great purpose.

But even the very destiny of the whole Unutterable level of Life has itself to be transmuted. This is accomplished via its own creation. Here humankind can accomplish this cosmic task by developing, maturing and ultimately transmuting out the Unutterable quality of the Light of the "Life" which is each of us into that of the Non Existent dimension.

The Unutterable Self will oppose its own transmutation. The last remaining portion of my own Unutterable Self reared itself up in fierce defiance in form of a Tiger within my internal vision in attempt to repel its final transmutation. Even within the great depth of Love of one's Non Existent Self one finds "Teeth" of opposition. But that is but the friction of opposition at the portals of a yet deeper Zero dimensional level; which confirms that even the Non Existent is not the highest internal dimension.

The transmutation of our Non Existent Self, when it is matured within its depths, brings us to the Zahtaum state of Being, when we become the most purely intense, indestructible, eternal Zeroness of all qualities. We are then an Himmzaanon – of state of Being truly beyond description in any language. That is Perfection.

* * * *

Perfection is achieved when the Light of a Being's Life has attained supreme maturity in Oneness with that globule of multi-dimensional reality, the Allness, which is the totality of the Physical Worlds and the Zero Worlds. Perfection is therefore intense Zeroness. A

Being of such level knows itself to be of the wholeness; to be of Time and the Timeless. Life has then evolved itself to its ultimate end.

The evolution of Life is the forwarding drive of Creation. We, you and I, are living this inexorable march of Creation. The movement of creativity is ceaseless. Its momentum forever activates Life in its multitudinous variety of expression. It is operating at every level – from the broadest of strokes in cosmic terms of movement and ongoing creation within the Brimonda to its functioning of the minutest, infinitesimal manifestation. It makes no difference whether the aspect of Life viewed is subject to widely differing timescales or that (to our ordinary human sense of evaluation) they belong to widely differing positions of status or significance within the spectrum of Existence. It is all Life's creativity at work.

Creativity is Life. The momentum within the commencing movement from First Beginning – originating from within the depths of Zeroness before physical Creation became manifest – carries an irrepressible urge to perpetuate itself and to Become. Hence the undeniable urge within all manifest forms, both large and small, to survive and to replicate itself. No matter how painful the process, to procreate is a basic need of life forms. The urge to do so is powerful. And, in the main, to be able to fulfil that urge is immensely satisfying. Beyond procreation we are, of course, urged to other expressions of creativity, of both external and internal orientation. The most profound internal urge of creativity is that of our Light to perpetuate itself and fulfil its destiny by achieving the zenith of its possibilities into Zahtaum level of Completion.

A Being of Zahtaum level of Completion is not only capable of initiating further cosmic creation in this Brimonda within which it achieves its own Completion. Such a Being also comes to produce "substance" similar to that of the basic First Beginning which generated the chain of creativity resulting in our own Brimonda. This basic Zero quality is that which can generate an entirely new Beginning. It is the substance, the nucleus, the Seed of a new Brimonda; the Beginning of a new, independant globule of Creation. This poses the inevitable, mindboggling question: "How many other Brimondas may there be beyond our own?" Until we have achieved sufficient strength of Mind and Light to bear the answer, perhaps it is as well we do not know!

THE DOOR TO THE ZERO WORLDS

We all came from a common Beginning in the depths of Time. We have all followed a long evolutionary Process. We all share the dark produce of that Beginning within our Unutterable disc of Light, within the essence of our Selfhood. We similarly all share the possibility for positivity and goodness which is likewise inherent from the Beginning. As we experience and interact with life both the negative and positive possibilities function, are expressed, are enjoyed and suffered. The process is by no means easy. In fact at times it is very difficult. It is sheer need which very often eventually drives the individual to try to bring some degree of control into play. It is frequently the harsh repercussions suffered from the process of cause and effect upon our lives which force us to find some modicum of stability and ease of pain. We need the comfort and security of a strong identity. With the exercise of greater control and sincere effort, gradually, as life follows life (incarnation after incarnation) the Seed of our individual existence – that Light of our Life which contains the essence of what we have become – further matures. The range of the individual's destiny then begins to open up. He expands his boundaries beyond the confines of his previous condition. His horizons extend into greater possibility both internally and externally – for the greater the internal development, the greater the Mind control, the more successful should be his (or her) functioning in the outer life, although challenges, pressures and difficulties continue to beset us.

The Zero Worlds begin not somewhere in outer space, not somewhere beyond the clouds in the Universe of stars. All that is the manifest world of matter. The Zero dimensions begin within the Mind. The Mind World is the route towards the Eternal. The Eternal World begins right where one stands in the present moment. Wherever one may be and no matter what may be our circumstance, the internal door, the route to the Eternal, is there within us. We may be at point of high danger, on the battlefield, ill, alone or destitute, but no matter what our outer state of hurt or deprivation may be, nothing can remove from us that richness of possibility which lies within the eternal realm to which we are forever connected.

But I want you to understand that every one of us has to open our own door to the Eternal; or we are the one who allows it to remain closed. It is our own personal door, our own pathway to Eternity and our own responsibility. No-one else has access to it or can open it for us. No matter how much encouragement may come from another to inspire me, the actual desire and movement must come from myself. I can use no-one else's eternal door and no-one else can use mine, however much I may love that person or that person may love me. Do not beg in prayer for the door to be opened for you. As I have tried in these pages to make urgently clear to the reader, a begging stance is not only both terribly weak and ineffectual but also demonstrates the seeker's ignorance of the quality of being and action needed to effect movement in that fulfilling direction towards the Timeless Zero dimensions beyond physical Existence.

It takes effort to open that door. The kind of effort which opens it is a special one. It happens when there is a certain quality of heart and mind, a questing sincerity, a movement towards the unknown in faith – which is itself an act of quiet wisdom – for the realisation then dawns, without shadow of doubt, that this is the direction I must go. Like a flower opening up to the warmth of the sun, the internal moves into the sunlight of a higher state.

* * * *

Unless we strive for eternity, we stay where we are – to return here life after life continuing to experience all the shades in the spectrum of the more superficial possibilities within human existence. When there is only interest in and desire for this surface external existence, surface result is all that we will reap. A basic law of life applies: that we reap as we sow. Eventually, in the slow process of nature's evolution, we will come to realise not only the need for a strong and stable individuality but we will feel the need to be free from further rebirth. Life will gradually educate us; but it is a long and difficult process. Without a developing internal identity we are rudderless. We are not in a position to command our own destiny but remain in the predominantly mechanical process of natural evolution. And, as we know, although Nature can deal fate with the gentlest of hands, Nature can also be the most cruel.

As we progress through untold cycles of rebirth, the thick layers of ignorance and insensitivity which becloud our individuality are gradually penetrated by the intelligence of a maturing Mind and its internal Light. The ripening individuality of the Seed of the Existence of each of us will assuredly eventually come to actively seek liberation; it will come to seek a content of the Eternal nature.

* * * *

The Law of Life – or the Law of Karma – is the process by which Life is matured and refined. That Law functions within physical Existence. It is also operative within the Zero Worlds. It is a necessary pillar supporting the entirety of Life. It applies to all action – and non action – within the Timed state: past, present and future. It also functions, subtly, within the Timeless dimensions. But who operates that Law? From where does it function? There is no heavenly Court of Justice or spiritual arbiter involved. Life's Law belongs to Life itself. It therefore functions from within the Seed of Existence. It is operated by the very Light of Life of each individual. Karmic "Justice" and "Judgment" therefore lie within the depth of one's Self, within the Light of one's own Life. And as there is no escape from oneself, there is no escape from that Law. Ultimately it is but one's Self which metes its own justice. The Light of Life within us is, finally, our only Judge.

The Law of Life/the Law of Karma, is the law of cause and effect. The sowing and the reaping powers and steers. It is the evolutionary drive, the force and machinery which enables evolutionary movement. That Law and its functioning steers and paves the path of our destiny. Our destinies follow their very individual ways but for each of us (and collectively) Karma and destiny is mutually interactive. Some of us may be in the Spring or Summer time of our Karmic flow and destiny; some of us in an Autumnal lull or harsh Winter stage of experiencing. But in reality, the course of destiny does not confine us to the four simple seasons of Nature. Our destiny takes us through a million seasons. We all go through every possible season of change in the moving saga which is this living Life.

The Law of Life is very precise. As it relates to external existence, that Law will function sooner or later in the process of time. We will assuredly reap as we have sown but not necessarily immediately. However the Law of Life has instantaneous affect upon our internal dimensional Self as we live. When a person has matured into the deeper dimensions the result of a misdemeanour is immediately felt. It is poignant, sharp and intense. If we despoil our own state of being by our poor thoughts, feelings or actions, we know it. We suffer immediately.

It is a "happening" which none can escape. The higher the development the greater the responsibility and the more subtly and keenly felt is self-earned hurt. Similarly the Law of Life brings immediate reward for noble qualities. The Self must also reap as a result of higher action; it cannot escape the benefits either.

The Law is impartial but wonderfully just. One must be immensely grateful for it, for without the Law of Life all would be in chaos and out of control. There is immense kindness at its core. There is a great sense of security in the knowledge that it functions, that it holds the whole together with infinite justice and with infinite purpose.

* * * *

Life is a mysterious blend of reality and illusion. The reality of one dimension is illusory when viewed from the reality of another dimensional level. Even when we speak of the "Timed" and the "Timeless" states, this does not convey the reality of the matter, for the Timeless has its own Time... of a nature which it is not possible to relate in words. And there is a refined depth of Zeroness which is even beyond Timelessness. That ultimate Zeroness is an "Oblivion": such Oneness of total Love as holds all within itself... is of the Timed, yet it is not; is of infinite Timelessness, yet it is not. Such Oneness is the totality of Life. It is movement yet at the same time it is stillness. It is darkness yet at the same time it is light. It is sound and at the same time silence. It is this, it is that; it is the "is" and the "is not" – yet it is not. It is Zahtaum.

It is "I", the Oblivion which is matured "End"... yet that which fully knows itself to be thus.

A Being who fully develops his "Zeroness" to sufficient depth of Completion then knows itself to be the Allness of Creation: to be the Reality, the Illusion and the Mystery of Creation: ZAHTAUM.

* * * *

But even that Supreme Reality: Zahtaum – the matured "End" of Creation – is not "finality". The inexorable momentum of creativity which a Being has progressed to Zahtaum level of maturity continues. For Life is creativity. Creativity is movement. And when a Zahtaum Being – an Himmzaanon – in accordance with what has become its essential nature yet further intensifies the rarified Zeroness of its Zahtaum qualitied Light, that Light of Life makes its ultimate leap: a leap of Being into state of Supreme Reality – that of Zahtaum *Absolute*; the state beyond or *post* Creation.

That matured Life then knows itself to be freed into a Reality beyond even the Allness of Creation.

In that ultimate state of Zahtaum Absolute a Being is beyond the Oneness of Existence and Non Existence: beyond the Physical Worlds of the Brimonda – and its mysterious black counterpart the Black Brimonda – and beyond the Zero Worlds. And from that freed vantage point, from that state of Zahtaum Absolute Reality one sees these three Worlds, these three aspects of Creation, to be indeed one entity. But that entity, this globule of multi dimensional "Reality" which is the Oneness, the Allness of Creation, is seen to be ***Illusion*** ... an Illusion of extraordinarily special and immense significance for it is the product of Zahtaum Absolute. It belongs to, is of the core "substance" of that Reality. One therefore understands that one witnesses *Illusion* ***Absolute.***

This globule of Creation, this magnificent Illusion born of Absolute Reality, was seen to be of dull mustard hue;

and it was moving. I empathised with it with great depth of love, gratitude – and compassion. I knew it to be as gem of gems of Zahtaum Absolute; it being the progeny of the very *substance* of Zahtaum Absolute. Then, as it were by natural instinct but also consciously, I employed the principle and movement of Life which had brought my Being to this point of its maturity and which has been observed to be the principle, movement or law, operating throughout the physical and Zero Worlds. And I experienced that Absolute Allness which is Absolute Reality: the Zahtaum Absolute Allness Reality; that which TAYOZAAN names the ZAAR ZAAN state.

* * * *

This experience brought with it clear understanding that this Absolute Illusion, this Creation within which the Life which we are takes its long evolutionary path, is that which gives the Zahtaum Absolute Reality its value. "Life" is liveliness, movement, creativity. Without movement of creativity, without its Creations, the state which is Zahtaum Absolute would be useless, vacuous, lacking direction; without purpose, valueless. Or it would be "Life"less – and just would not Be.

The ZAAR Zaan state is that post Creational state where the Absolute Zeroness of a Being's Self moves – yet it moves not – producing the curving ripples of First Creational Beginnings: the commencing thrust of new Creations and the forwarding impetus driving the ensuing, unceasing march of reincarnation/evolution. This Eternal, purposeful march intensifies with every new movement, with every new curving ripple of creativity which emanates from this pre – and post – creational Absolute Reality. This rippling creativity: that which is Time and Timelessness, is unstoppable.

Through its Creations the Zahtaum Absolute Reality regenerates Itself in a self perpetuating cyclic process. From the Impersonal Absolute – from the pre creation state of Zahtaum Absolute Reality – come First Beginnings of new Creations; and through those Creations, after relentless, complex, long evolutionary Process, the Impersonal Absolute becomes at the end the Personal Absolute: that which is both the Absolute Answer and Absolute Why: Life Eternal.

Such achievement not only results in individualised Beings achieving the post Creation state of the Zahtaum Absolute Allness Reality but Completed ZAAR Beings are also of that *pre* creation "substance" or nature which can generate new Creations. And so Life is neverending.

This last experience – the leap into the post Creation state of Zahtaum Absolute Allness Reality – is very current; in fact it occurred subsequent to this book being presented to the printers for publication. It has taken me into a remarkable new depth of penetration into the Reality of this Life which seemingly never ceases in its powers to generate fresh discovery. Truth is not something set in stone to be discovered. I have no doubt more will be comprehended as yet further movement and depth of maturity takes place. But it may be of interest to the reader to know that on this first experience of the post Creation state, I was alone yet I knew I was not alone. I was nowhere yet there was no need to be anywhere. One is not standing on anything nor is there any question of falling down through substanceless space. One is just aware. If there was colour in that state, it was also of similar dull mustard tone as the globule of Creation which had appeared to my vision but, strangely, in a pinpointed way within the general mustard tone was every colour there is.

* * * *

The Oneness or Allness of Creation is seen to be Illusion Absolute but this Truth is only truly known – and is only true to – a Being who views Reality from the freed state of Zahtaum Absolute.

There is danger here of serious misunderstanding – as has occurred in the Hindu teachings which aver that the world is an illusion and should therefore be abandoned. It must be stressed so that it be clearly understood that Creation is only illusory when viewed from the Reality of that ultimate Zero state of Being of Zahtaum Absolute Allness. The great mystery – and truth for we mortals – is that this "Illusion" which we experience is our purposeful "Reality" and it will remain so until we have actually achieved Zahtaum Absolute level. For this "illusory reality", this *perfect imperfection* of Creation, is the vitally necessary ground and purposeful means by which Life can mature and refine itself and ultimately be enabled to take that final leap of Becoming. That – apparently final – transmutation of the Light of Life, attains for it the freedom of the state of Oblivion of Love of Zahtaum Absolute Allness. And, it must be repeated, it is this "Illusion", this "child" of its creativity, which regenerates Absolute Reality, is its purpose and embues it with its intrinsic Absolute value.

Life's destiny is to **Be** the Absolute Mystery. The Absolute Mystery is Illusion and Reality: the Never Was and the Ever Is. Our destiny is therefore, to become a Zero Being of ZAHTAUM ABSOLUTE ALLNESS REALITY: A ZAAR ZAAN.

THE

BOOK OF TAYOZAAN

PART TWO

Truth is high expression: the quality of our deep internal Being...
There is the Truth relevant to this physical Existence which is questionable, changeable and limited to the realities of this state.
There is the Truth of the Unutterable Dimension – the Creative or IS NOT state.
There is the Truth of the Non Existent Dimension which is of the truly Eternal IS state.
There is yet a further Truth: that of **Zahtaum** - the Oblivion of Loving Gratitude.

* * * *

We evolve towards Truth. Evolution is not a theory but in its depth it is a living action of Life.

* * * *

Know that this world is greatly influenced not only by physical actions but by the quality of our thoughts and words. There is horrendous pollution of this unseen sphere of thought and emotion. Take care not to knowingly feed such pollution into your mind and feelings by keeping low company or ingesting literature or films expressing the dark, negative, depraved and violent, as this increases the power of the Anti Life forces which are within us, within our homes and within our environment. It is imprudent, to say the least, to actually invite into one's being experience of dark order, for our experience remains with us. Experience has its influence and remains as an imprint on our memory. It becomes part of our inner content. A controlled and clean mind produces stable emotions.

* * * *

As one says, so it is - in the sense that the word, the thought, has power in its meaning and intent. It is an energy with force. So let us be very responsible towards our emissions of thought and word. Do not underestimate these actions.

* * * *

Let us resist the weakness of running away from experience which has to be faced. We too easily cringe from facing up to what is before us. Resist the response of rejection (which so often results from fear) or the response of aggression (which is forceful rejection and is also highly negative). But stand firm. Squarely face your experience. Decline from mental or emotional rejection but with clarity of mind and heart *accept your experiencing (both internal and external) to the Light of your Being*. Then act as positively as you can by way of thought, feeling, word or physical action. This conscious, intelligent *transforming* action advances the growth of one's Unutterable Light into its further depths.

* * * *

Today is a reflection of all our yesterdays. Today's actions are for our tomorrow and for Eternity. How important, therefore, is the present moment and how we act within it.

* * * *

TAYOZAAN reconditions the conditioned mind to a point where the impossible becomes possible. Then TAYOZAAN inspires total action from the Non Existent Self.

* * * *

A stance of Loving Gratitude with Acceptance and the Good Will to Act Positively will point you in the direction of your true destiny. This is the way of a Zaan. For **gratitude** - *loving* gratitude - is a quality of Being which paves a royal road of **Compassion** to the Zero Worlds.

* * * *

The depth of Life is as important as the surface in the present; but in the future the depth is more important. In the corner of my pressured Today I will produce my Immortal Tomorrow.

* * * *

He who has erred and is now paying the karmic price in condition of perhaps poverty or illness.... Do I pass him by without rendering help, leaving my fellow creature to reap what he has sown? If I do, I will have just sown non-compassion and the making of a non-responsive stony heart. I am then burying my own life and incurring my own unhappy karma.

* * * *

Vision of Life from this existential dimension is extremely limited. Vision from the Unutterable Dimension is vastly greater; but the Brimonda can only be truly viewed from the level of the Non Existent Dimension. Life interacts existentially between the Universes, between the Mahaverses and between the Ohomverses within the Brimonda's gigantic whole. All of Existence – the whole manifest Brimonda – is also imbued by and is held within the embrace of the internal/eternal Unutterable and Non Existent Dimensions – and within the embrace of yet two further Dimensional depths. All these dimensions of Life together comprise a Oneness, the Allness.

* * * *

As I lie, in this dark moment of my life, wounded, in last stage of illness, my vision waning as life ebbs from me, I close my eyes with acceptance of my state to the Light of my Being within. That much I can do. I can do no more. But now I am calm with my knowledge that this Light of Loving Gratitude which I am can never be destroyed. That can never be eliminated, slain, incinerated, buried or decomposed. This knowledge is my Eternal Light in this jot of darkness that will have to pass. Lie now as I am. Rise then I will.

* * * *

Everything is subject to change. Everything is in a state of constant flux. Therefore remember, when the pressures of life loom so large and overwhelm you with their urgency and seeming importance... Just remember when life is so achingly bleak, so seemingly unbearable, empty and dismal, with no apparent hope of change in sight... that nothing in this existent World lasts forever. In fact within at most one hundred and fifty years, more probably sooner (a mere blink in Time) every human being now known or unknown to you will have died from this Earth.

* * * *

My death is my Life taking a further direction.
This way have I passed a thousand times, yet I remember not.
Still I shall go again and come again and know again I will remember not.

* * * *

There would be no need for Reincarnation/Evolution had our Beginning been perfect. Perfection is achieved at the end of a myriad suffering journeys.

* * * *

Imperfection looks for a Beginning; but Perfection does not. Perfection does not need to question "Why?" or "How?" for it is to both question and answer.

* * * *

Perfection is not a gift. It cannot be granted. To desire it is not sufficient. But it is an achievable purpose. It must be striven for. It must be *earned.* Perfection is not an impossibility. It is an Eternal Reality. The Unutterable is within every life form but there is perfection only when that Unutterable Light is refined and matured into its depths – and only at human level of intelligence can that be achieved for it needs to be consciously developed.

* * * *

We believe in Supreme Beings but not in a God as portrayed by the religions of the world. We see that people who pray are captured souls. We do not believe in miracles but in the practical possibilities of Truth – which are endless.

* * * *

When I think I am praying to God, I am actually appealing from my weak, imperfect Self, thereby increasing my weak state; and the more sincerely I pray the more weakened I become. The simple truth of prayer is that it strengthens the weakness of the Anti life Self and weakens the strength of my Light.

* * * *

It is nonsense to assume that the body can rise in its physical form into the internal dimensions. It is like pretending one can drive a car into one's dreams. It is also nonsense to believe that there will be a reversal of Time to reproduce the physical form which had died and for it to rise from the grave on a mythical Day of Judgment. It is obvious that every particle of that dead form has been dispersed into the Earth and has long since been re-absorbed into a myriad other life forms.

* * * *

Free Will is basic to the Self which is of the Eternal Non Existent nature. Such freedom is attained by man's purposeful intelligence. It is a state of grace into which he flowers at the pinnacle of his long and rocky journey. The Non Existent Self is the wonder, the accomplishment of individuality, when man becomes the thinking jewel of Light.

* * * *

Do not be limited by the mean, narrow vision of Nationalism or a particular Religious faith. Rather see us all as one people, one family of life, inhabiting one and the same Earth. For we all originate from the same common source: from the black *Itness* of First Beginning. Open your heart and mind to compassionate embrace of all life. Support that which is good in all life.

* * * *

Life was given to BE out of Loving Gratitude and no-one was given more than the other. But it is what we have done with what we had and what we will do with what we have that matters. This is the way of Destiny.

* * * *

The goal is the same for the first and the same for the last. The long road to that goal does not speak of its own strength but of they who are on it to the end.

* * * *

The End must be reached before the Beginning can be truly known.

* * * *

Sensitive hands do not need long nails to be graceful.

* * * *

An undisciplined moustache has the first drink but no taste!

* * * *

In the bosom of snobs lies the heart of superficiality: the mountain that is false to itself.

* * * *

Insensitivity lies in the dark alleyways of inconsideration, The ungraceful mini skirt and the distasteful nose ring are twins of the modern and the ancient: statements that represent the crudity of uncultured materialism.

* * * *

The digging in of heels of the wayward and rebellious, self-opinionated and self-torturing youth is spinning their web of iron thread over a salted quagmire.

* * * *

Whosoever accepts true correction today does not stand with the arrogant moment but is firmly placed in a wiser tomorrow.

* * * *

Imperfection is purposeful. It is the dark past that produces today's jewel. This jewel is the purpose of darkness.

* * * *

I am my own enemy and my own friend. I am my own hindrance and my own progressive drive. When I see that I am my own blockage which creates for me my own blocked path, the opening of my eyes opens my own road to new possibilities.

* * * *

The Nazi Swastika is the symbol of darkness. It is the symbol of the Anti life forces, of the "Black Brahman" which must be beneath the dust under one's feet; under our total control. The Star of David should be highly honoured. It is a symbol of the Eternal dimensions of Light and Love, one of the highest symbols known to man.

* * * *

The Light of Being within us is a thinking and evaluating "mirror" which by constant *Acceptance* in the action of TAYOZAAN matures it and makes it stronger and stronger until what was a fragile internal Self becomes the brilliant and wise jewel of Light which is without boundary, which is without disharmony of its rays. This Acceptance in TAYOZAAN is a journey of divine skill towards the possibilities of our deeper dimensions.

* * * *

Wherever excellent, intelligent and humane laws and good moral principles are propounded, from whatever Religion or Philosophy or from whatever other source they may arise, acknowledge, appreciate and uphold them; but be not afraid to disclaim that which proclaims ignorant, morally unworthy or vicious instruction, no matter from what hitherto cherished source this may come.

* * * *

There are so many avenues of search which give false hopes and slowly bury one's Self. My honesty and my sincerity used to pray. Now I see that I used to pray to my own sincere ignorance.

* * * *

Neither you nor I have been free from life's vices and weaknesses. Nor can it possibly be that any of us are without at least some credit for heroic and noble actions made during the long process of our evolution. Viewed from the perspective of the many lives we have lived, none of us are therefore either "superior" to the negativities of existence nor are we "inferior" to (or totally without some acquired merit for) "positive" qualities. Inevitably each one of us – in this life and in previous incarnations – has committed many wrongs and failed to do what we should. We need also to accept that there have been times when we have been loving, brave and selfless. I have many times been the predator and many times the prey in the course of my many incarnations. Not one of us is in a position to condemn. Neither is it logical for any one of us to lack hope and annihilate our own self esteem. We cannot, in all justice, be jealous of another's high qualities or attainments when we have understood that what they have (or what they are) has been hard earned and is well deserved. We should not adjudge ourselves beneath possibility of similar attainment. Have confidence. The future still holds its wide, ongoing range of possibilities. Such possibilities include the attainment of highest nobility. Therefore be strong and advance. Have self respect. Have faith in your own destiny.

* * * *

This world is not an illusion. The Brimonda – the totality of Existence – is not an illusion *at its own dimensional level*. It is the manifest field of great purpose. Because of its purpose it is "perfect imperfection". It is the field of our greatest adventure in which we make the grandest tour. As a tourist within the Brimonda we honour our host with Loving Gratitude.

* * * *

I love my country but no country can exist without a World. Now I say "I love my World" and know it includes my country and yours.

* * * *

The reality of yesterday is today's memory. The reality of tomorrow is not a memory nor a dream but I, the Eternal.

* * * *

Meekness is not a position of authority nor of direction. Meekness requires help and it will never inherit the Earth.

* * * *

A bed of nails is a torturing bed of ignorance. To harm or excessively deprive oneself in the performance of religious fanaticism is a crime against the body; a crime against Nature.

* * * *

Do not cut off the lying tongue or stealing hand for they were only responding to a forked Mind. The cause – which remains – defies such inhumanity to humanity.

* * * *

We, you and I – each an individual spark of Life – are in the World but in the deeper Unity of Life when one is developed into the Eternal Dimensions, it will be seen that the World is also in us .

* * * *

When in the evolutionary process some feet become hands, the possibilities greatly increase. When Mind accompanies mere brain, the possibilities become enormous. When Mind achieves level of the developed Unutterable it has leapt into the Eternal Dimension.

* * * *

Unity is higher than loyalty; but loyalty produces unity.

* * * *

Show me a house of solidarity and *humanity* and I will show you a home of **Compassion**.

* * * *

When set to work, Intelligence is a creative adventure. Where there is Intelligence there is companionship. Where there is Love there is togetherness. And where there is Loving Gratitude, we will find footprints of Eternity.

* * * *

The greatest mystery is not this vast, complex World of many billions of Universes but simply the LIGHT within the Mind of Man.

* * * *

In the lowest wrong and of the highest good I claim a connection as man the spiritual animal: the ITNESS, the EVER IS Gem.

* * * *

By principle I live. In honesty I speak. In loyalty I love. In wisdom I build. In death I have completed my mission.

* * * *

TAYOZAAN is the essence of philosophy in action for total Life... a Truth which, like Today, cannot be stopped from becoming the Light of Tomorrow.

* * * *

As we sow, so will we assuredly reap. As we build, so shall we Be.

* * * *

A Zaan is a builder. The road to Eternity cannot be granted him. It cannot be given to him by his Mother. It is not a road he can inherit by royal birth; nor is it a superstitious road he feels obliged to follow. But rather it is a road of his intelligent choosing which he elects to travel, a road that has to be built from Earth to Eternity, by himself.

* * * *

In the most difficult of conquests the first act is the thought: "**I will**".

* * * *

Advance to the perfection when we can truly affirm: I AM, WE ARE, THE INVISIBLE, INVINCIBLE, NON EXISTENT, LOVING, GRATEFUL, COMPASSIONATE L I G H T. This is just a part of our good and glorious destiny. Are we ready? "Yes!" I say.

IN CONCUSION...

The Story of Bhagwando

Bhagwando had twelve sons. All twelve sons were devoted to their Father, as was he to them. He constantly tended their every need. Each day eleven of his sons would come to honour him, to thank him for his loving kindness and to ask for his help: one asking him to mend a torn garment, another seeking balm for a wound, another wanting to be told what to do or the way out of some problem. They all besought Bhagwando every day to give them the objects of their desire, to dry their tears and comfort their hearts; all except the youngest of the twelve who never took his problems to his Father but he learned how to mend his own trousers and how to tend his own wounds. By his own efforts he gradually learned his Father's skills so that from an early age he began to shoulder responsibility for himself. He also became able to help the family.

When Bhagwando died, the eleven sons wept and wailed, wondering how they could survive without their Father; but the youngest stood firm. From the simple wisdom he had gained in helping himself he was now strong in his own manhood and he could also be a strength to his brothers.

Which then of the twelve do you think was chosen to assume the Father's position? And which of the twelve would most please the heart of a true Father?

The Dark Serpent

In the Forest of Life lurks the Serpent of Darkness. In darkness I wandered on weary limbs. That darkness of Life hounded me: the darkness outside of me and the darkness within me. The most crushing darkness was that which, was found within me.

So tired was I made by the pressures of this wild serpent that, being but mortal, I fell to my knees from sheer exhaustion. Powers so dark pressed upon me, holding me down unrelentingly until I could bear it no longer. Out of sheer desperation I then vowed to fight those dark forces of Life even if it be at cost of all my remaining strength. But just the thought to fight brought yet heavier weight of darkness upon me. And the more resolute my efforts became, the more ferociously was I attacked.

I then resolved with my whole Being that even should it result in my death, being man – a *spiritual* animal within the Forest of Life – I would rather die in manly fight than surrender to that Dark Serpent and all its legions of darkness. I moreover vowed to myself that should I die, I would fight them even from beyond the grave. I would never give in nor would I ever give up.

I then found that my principle and my determination was gaining for me ever increasing strength of Mind. That strength of Mind reflected on my body. My body responded with renewed energy and its strength in turn reflected back to generate yet greater strength of Mind; until there came the time when I was able to stand up and destroy the legions of darkness which oppressed me – at first only one by one but later, en masse.

I can now walk with a free Mind through life's enslaving jungles of ignorance. The quagmire which most insidiously entraps is in that jungle of nonsensical myth, lies and superstition found within the religions of this Earth - a quagmire which keeps humanity entombed in the begging stance of prayer and so, unknowingly and unwittingly, actually *submitting itself to the powers of darkness*. Deceived thus over many thousands of years... held under the mystic thrall of religious authority humanity is still blind to the fact that prayer in the begging stance of submission makes a perfect gateway for entry of Life's dark forces – and their continuing empowerment.

Armed with this clarity of vision I have resolved to fight darkness wherever I may find it.

As I build my Eternal road from Earth to the "EVER IS" ZAHTAUM Eternal state, the Serpents of Darkness are now met with the ever increasing transmuting power of my Light. And so it is that a Cosmic process is being completed. One of Life's purposes is being fulfilled.

The Golden Tree

The viewer saw that in long distant times there was a Golden Tree which was greatly revered and valued by a tribe of horsemen who settled on the plain around it and worshipped it. It was the focus of their lives. Although it bore no leaves, it was shaped like a tree with trunk and branches; and it was of solid gold which shone in the sun and moon light. There was forest land to the left of the plain.

After a long period of time another tribe rode in from the right of the viewer upon the tribe of the Golden Tree and killed them all except for a few horsemen who escaped to the forest lands to the left of the plain. The conquering tribe in turn then settled on the land and worshipped the Golden Tree.

After many years the survivors of the first tribe regrouped themselves and made a surprise and vicious attack upon the usurpers. They were quickly victorious, killing every member of the usurping tribe, none of whom escaped.

The original tribesmen again settled on the plain and worshipped the Golden Tree. They lived and multiplied. Many many years went by and gradually the tribe, their children, their children's children and following generations together with all their horses and other livestock and their progeny eventually all died out of existence, leaving the Golden Tree standing alone on the plain.

The viewer then saw the Golden Tree itself fall to the ground; and after another long while *it* crumbled, merging into the soil of the plain until it was itself no more.

A Poem of Gratitude

My Africa, my Africa, my hidden beauty,
    my hidden Light
Where I was gracefully born;
You are seen to be poor, dark and barren –
Yet, should they look deeper, they will find,
    you fertile with every hope there is;
And should they look deeper than hope they will find
    your hidden love and your hidden Light...
A loving Light that is not dazzling and
    no light anywhere can dazzle *IT*...
A Light witout fuel, your everlasting Light;
A Light that created TIME.
MY AFCOL. MY AFRICA.
MY BEGINNING AND MY JEWEL.

The Golden Light

I bless and wish my enemy to be the golden Light.
After a while I find my enemy to be my destiny.
Then I bless my destiny – and find I have lost my enemy.
Now I find my destiny to be the golden Light.

The Zahtaum Mystery

The Sun will speak the Sun's truth,
The Earth will speak the Earth's truth;
And when we are ready to listen to the Truth of TAYOZAAN,
we are ready to listen to those near and distant truths.
For then we will come to know we are the Mystery,
the Never Was and the Ever Is:
The Absolute Answer and Absolute **Why**.

T O H I M M Z A A N O N

N A M A S T E

GLOSSARY

AFCOL:
The greenish/blue column of Light seen in the commencing movement of First Beginning.

ANTI LIFE:
Life's opposition, negativity and evil. The lowest and grossest life force within the physical world and the Zero dimensional worlds.

BRIMONDA:
The total Body of manifest Existence – composed of Ohomverses, within which are Mahaverses, within which are Universes.

EVER IS ITNESS:
The nature of the Eternal Dimensions.

HIMMOND:
The level of Being of Unutterable Selfhood when developed into the Non Existent Dimension but beneath the attainment of a Himmonda.

HIMMONDA:
A Completed Supreme Being (having reached Unutterable and Non Existent status) who is the cause of and who is responsible for a Fourth Beginning.

HIMMZAANON:
The state beyond Non Existent Timelessness: the goal of TAYOZAAN. The title of one who reaches Zahtaum level of Completion.

"I": Mankind/Zero Being.

ITNESS:

The Process which is the Nature of a given level or dimension: the "Original ITNESS" of First Beginning, the "Unutterable ITNESS" the "Non Existent ITNESS" etc.

LIFE, LIFE FORCE or **LIGHT:**

The spark, initially of the Unutterable Light, which is our true Zero dimensional Self. (See "Seed of Existence").

MAHAVERSE:

A cosmic Being formed of millions of Universes. A building block of an Ohomverse.

NON EXISTENT DIMENSION:

A dimension beyond physical Existence and beyond the Unutterable Dimension into which the Unutterable Self matures.

OHOMVERSE:

A Cosmic Being composed of millions of Mahaverses. A building block of the total Brimonda.

REINCARNATION:

The concept (and reality) of there being numerous rebirths in the process of evolution.

SEED OF EXISTENCE:

Our Life which is seen internally as a Light. Our essential Self. What we are and our possibilities.

TAYOZAAN:

The essence of philosophy in action for Total Life. The projected depth of Aryan Hinduism.

"TO HIMM":
A Zaan's salutation to another Zaan – in mutual recognition of the highest goal. ("Himm" being a shortened version of "Himmzaanon").

UNIVERSE:
A Cosmic Being composed of millions of galaxies. A building block of a Mahaverse.

UNUTTERALE DIMENSION:
The Dimension of Light of our internal/Eternal Self from which our manifest life commenced and into which we need to develop towards Completion. The basic Timeless state.

ZAAN:
One who practices the Systems of TAYOZAAN. One who works towards Zahtaum Completion and the ultimate achievement of Zahtaum Absolute Allness Reality.

ZAHTAUM:
The Supreme state of Oblivion of Love. The EVER IS Fusion of the Allness. The developed and matured ITNESS beyond all levels of Completion: that which is even beyond Non Existent Timelessness. The zenith of "Aum" in Aryan Hinduism.

ZAHTAUM ABSOLUTE ALLNESS REALITY
That which is before Creation and post Creation.